Ancient Peoples and Places

THE CITY OF CONSTANTINOPLE

General Editor

DR. GLYN DANIEL

ABOUT THE AUTHOR

Michael Maclagan was educated at Winchester and Christ Church, Oxford, where he took a First Class Honours Degree in Modern History in 1935. A Lecturer at Christ Church from 1937 to 1939, he was later elected Fellow of Trinity College, Oxford, becoming successively Dean, Librarian and Senior Tutor. Following service in the Army during World War II, he was appointed University Lecturer in Modern History at Oxford.

Mr. Maclagan, who has made a point of visiting Istanbul at least once a year since 1955, has read and lectured widely on Byzantine art and history, and helped to organize the Thirteenth International Byzantine Congress at Oxford in 1966.

Ancient Peoples and Places

THE CITY OF
CONSTANTINOPLE

Michael Maclagan

67 PHOTOGRAPHS
22 LINE DRAWINGS
I MAP

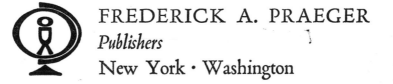

FREDERICK A. PRAEGER
Publishers
New York · Washington

THIS IS VOLUME SIXTY IN THE SERIES

Ancient Peoples and Places

GENERAL EDITOR: DR. GLYN DANIEL

BOOKS THAT MATTER

Published in the United States of America in 1968
by Frederick A. Praeger, Inc., Publishers
111 Fourth Avenue, New York, N.Y. 10003.
Library of Congress Catalog Card Number: 67–28193
Printed in Holland

CONTENTS

5

ILLUSTRATIONS

To my Wife my Companion in many Byzantine Travels

Introduction

I OFFER NO APOLOGY FOR prolonging the history of Constantinople from Byzantine into Turkish times. The noble panorama of the city today owes more to its Ottoman rulers than to the Greek emperors. The two cultures are intermingled in the sphere of art and related in the world of history.

Orthography offers an almost insoluble problem. After much hesitation, I have preserved the Latin form for the names of people – the Emperor Heraclius (not Heraklios) and the Patriarch Sergius (not Sergios) – but I have kept the Greek forms for local place names – Bosporos or Kainourgion; in particular I have chosen the forms Hagia Sophia and Eirene for the two churches of the Holy Wisdom and the Holy Peace. For Turkish names, I have sought to give the spellings in use today, which might assist an actual visitor, even though this involved replacing the familiar 'Pasha' by 'Paşa'. In modern Turkish, C is pronounced as the J in 'jam'; Ç as in 'church': Ş as in 'shield': Ö and Ü as they are in German: the undotted I is not unlike the U in further: commonsense will cover the rest. Thus CAMI (mosque – which becomes CAMII if preceded by a personal name) appears in French books as DJAMI.

In Turkey itself an initial I, as in Istanbul, has a dot above it.

I wish I could thank all the friends who have helped me towards some understanding of the Byzantine world. Among the dead, I honour particularly Thomas Whittemore, Royall Tyler and my father. Among the living, I am bound to thank David Talbot Rice, with memories going back to the darker days of the war, and more friends in Oxford than I can name. In Turkey I would like to thank Professor Eyice, of the University of Istanbul, Dr Feridun Diremtekin, of the Museum of Ayasofya, Dr Nezih Fıratlı of the Archaeological Museum, and Mr Ernest Hawkins. Many unknown Turks have helped me with true kindness as I sought the remoter traces of Byzantium in modern Istanbul. Finally, I would like to thank Mr Kenneth Swan, under whose flag I have seen many otherwise inaccessible remains of this glorious and enduring civilization.

The lines from W.B. Yeats at the head of Chapter V come from an early draft of his poem 'Sailing to Byzantium', and I am grateful to Professor A. Norman Jeffares for permission to quote them from his article in the *Review of English Studies* XXII (1946).

In my choice of illustrations I have tried to show some of the less frequented churches and mosques, while still doing justice to the well-known ones. The keen eye of my wife has saved me from many mistakes and inconsistencies, for which I am truly grateful.

M.M.

CHAPTER I

Byzantium

The site of Byzantium is as regards the sea more favourable to security and prosperity than that of any city in the world known to us ... The Greeks, then, would entirely lose all this commerce or it would be quite unprofitable to them, if the Byzantines were disposed to be deliberately unfriendly to them.   POLYBIUS IV, 38

THE CITY OF CONSTANTINE has indeed a noble situation. Its position is triangular; on the west is the land of Thrace, on the south is the Sea of Marmara and to the north-east the wonderful, deep, sea-water harbour called the Golden Horn. And northwards from the tip of the city runs the narrow thoroughfare of the Bosporos, dividing Europe from Asia and joining the Black Sea, fed by the great traffic-carrying rivers of Russia, to the Sea of Marmara, and thence, through the historic narrows, flanked by Gallipoli and Troy, to the Mediterranean and the world beyond.

Fig. 1

The importance of this dramatic site was not immediately realized. During the seventh century BC the cities of Greece were busily employed in planting colonies in this area, but Cyzicus and Lampsacus had both become important before Byzantium was founded; and so had Chalcedon, on the Asiatic side of the Bosporos. Indeed Herodotus tells us that the start of Chalcedon antedated that of Byzantium by seventeen years; both were begun by Megara, a city on the Greek mainland midway between Athens and Corinth. According to tradition Byzantium was founded in the first half of the seventh century BC, perhaps in 658 and by a leader called Byzas. Both traditions have been disputed; and recent archaeological researches put the establishment of the city a generation later. John the Lydian (a historian writing in the middle of the sixth century after Christ) states categorically that the city was founded in 628 BC and by a certain Zeuxippus. Herodotus also informs us that

Megabazus, a Persian general, observed that the people of Chalcedon (the modern Kadiköy) must have been blind to miss the superior position across the water. In later years this judgement was appropriated by the priests of the shrine of Apollo at Delphi. Both Strabo and Tacitus recount that the expedition from Megara consulted the oracle there before setting out and were instructed to build 'opposite to the land of the blind men'.

In any case, by 600 BC there was a city already beginning to flourish which had for its acropolis, or citadel, the high ground on which now stand the Palace of the Sultans and the great church of Hagia Sophia. The arrival of the Greeks does not necessarily mean that this prepossessing position was hitherto unoccupied; it has been suggested that there may have been a Phrygian settlement on the same hill, responsible for pottery remains which have been discovered some five feet below the church of Hagia Eirene. But the splendour of the existing buildings makes it unlikely that the archaeological history of this area can ever be fully explored.

As trade developed between the world of the Black Sea and that of the Aegean, the city of Byzantium prospered. In addition to the strength of its position, the country round about was fertile and the neighbouring seas were full of fish – as they are still today. Indeed the natural harbour of the Golden Horn seems first to have been valued from a piscatorial rather than a commercial angle. Such a site was coveted. In 506 BC Byzantium was captured by the Medes; in 478 it was freed by the Spartan Pausanias. From then on the place was involved in the numerous wars which beset Greece and emphasized the political disunity which went with the brilliance of Hellenic thought and art. For most of the fifth century Byzantium was linked to Athens, but in 411 the city reverted to Sparta. The connection seems to have been unpopular, for when in 408 the agile but undisciplined genius of Alcibiades was besieging the city, some

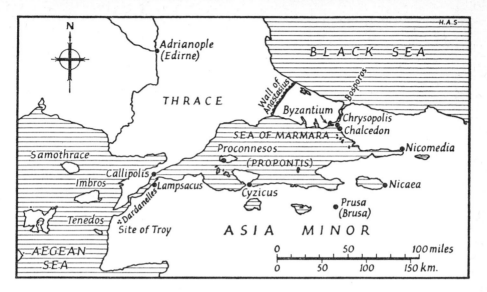

Fig. 1 *Byzantium and its surroundings*

of the Byzantines opened the gates to him. Five years later a great Spartan sea victory restored Byzantium to their power. It was therefore to a Spartan fortress that Xenophon led the weary survivors of the 10,000 when they crossed the Bosporos and re-entered Europe in 400. Their reception was unsatisfactory, and it was only the persuasive tact of Xenophon which prevented the Greeks from looting Byzantium.

In the fourth century BC Byzantium began with an alliance with Ephesus, Rhodes and Samos, turned again to Athens, transferred her loyalty to Thebes, rejoined Athens and endured (in 340) a siege by Philip of Macedon. His failure was attribut-ed to the goddess Hecate, and by a sinister foreshadowing the coinage of Byzantium displayed in her honour a crescent and a star. The vast campaigns of Philip's son, the great Alexander, passed Byzantium by; but in their dispersal of Greek ideas and Greek art they may be regarded as laying in some sense the foundations of the later Roman Empire. For while the states of

15

Greece were in decline, the power of Rome was slowly growing outwards. Somewhere about 150 BC Byzantium made a
treaty with Rome, and became a free city, paying tribute, on the
margins of the Latin world. In AD 53 this tribute was remitted
for five years (it is in connection with this that Tacitus tells the
story of the Delphic Oracle); but by then the political brilliance
of Augustus had moulded Republican Rome into a Mediterranean empire.

SEVERUS
In AD 73 Vespasian incorporated Byzantium into that em-
pire, and there is little to tell until the end of the second century.
The death of Commodus left the throne vacant and the An-
tonine dynasty extinct. C. Pescennius Niger, the Governor of
Syria, was proclaimed Emperor, but so was Septimius Severus.
The latter triumphed, but the people of Byzantium opted for
Pescennius. Severus besieged the town for most of three years
from autumn, 193. In 196 it fell and paid the penalty. The magnificent walls, so well made that they seemed of one stone, were
destroyed and the city sacked. None the less the position was
too important to neglect, and after an interval Severus began to
rebuild the city and the walls; his reconstruction made possible
the urban opportunity which was to catch the eye of Constantine the Great. Severus gave Byzantium the name of Antoninia
but it did not endure.

Fig. 3
The city laid out by Severus was larger than the former Byzantium. Its walls ran from near the Galata Bridge of today to
the column of Constantine (not then erected) and then followed the contours of the hill round the southern end of the Hippodrome to reach the sea of Marmara east of Hagia Sophia.
Where today is the open space between Hagia Sophia and the
Blue Mosque was a fine square, called the Tetrastoös. Adjacent
to these were the Hippodrome itself and the baths of Zeuxippus
(the name traditionally a contraction of Zeus patron of horses,
a powerful Thracian cult). A great street led westwards from
the Tetrastoös to the main gate. Hence ran the great military

highway, the Via Egnatia leading to Thessalonica, to Dyr-
rhachium and across the Adriatic to Rome itself.

On the top of the hill stood various temples. Excavations
conducted between the later churches of Hagia Sophia and
Hagia Eirene revealed shrines of Artemis under the former, of
Aphrodite under the latter, and of Apollo between them. Little
remains of the work of Severus. Some of the under-structure
of the Hippodrome is no doubt his work, though it was enlarged by Constantine. There is however a pillar, usually called
the Column of the Goths, in the Park below the Saray, which
may be associated with a theatre constructed in that area by
Severus. Its date and builder are uncertain; by some it has been
associated with Claudius II (268–70), by others with Constantine. The single inscription tersely thanks Fortune for successful
campaigns against the Goths.

For Byzantium the third century after Christ passed quietly;
for the Roman Empire as a whole it was a time of crisis. Unmemorable and shadowy emperors, promoted by the army,
came and went, and particularly in the west there were economic difficulties and a decline of population. And on all the frontiers of the Empire was a growing threat from the barbarian
peoples. Two remarkable men strove to resolve this crisis. Diocletian (284–305) made the decision that the task of ruling was
too much for one man: he envisaged one emperor in the west
and another in the east. To each would be assigned a second-in-
command with the rank of Caesar and the promise of succession. It was hoped that the two Augusti would choose their
Caesars by merit rather than kinship and that the intervention
of the legions would be avoided; the hope was vain. Diocletian
also greatly augmented the ritual surrounding the person of the
emperor.

Rome was the natural capital of the western half of the Empire, though its administration made increasing use of Milan

Plate 1

DIOCLETIAN

17

Fig. 2   Gold solidus showing head of Constantine the Great

and Trier and later of Ravenna. But Diocletian did not fix on a centre for the eastern sector, which he had reserved for himself and which included the Balkan Peninsula, Asia Minor, Syria and Egypt. His most frequent place of residence was Nico-media, the modern Izmit, at the head of an inlet on the south shore of the sea of Marmara, where he had first proclaimed him-self Emperor. Almost alone among great dictators Diocletian had the courage to retire (305) and devoted the last decade of his life to gardening (in circumstances of considerable luxury) at Split. It was left to the imperious figure of Constantine to continue his work, after a period of further disorders.

CHAPTER II

The City of Constantine

The conqueror bequeathed to his family the inheritance of the Roman empire; a new capital, a new policy and a new religion; and the innovations which he established have been embraced and consecrated by succeeding generations...the advantageous position of Constantinople, which appears to have been formed by nature for the centre and capital of a great monarchy.   E. GIBBON, *Decline and Fall of the Roman Empire*, Ch. XVII.

CONSTANTINE is one of the epic figures of true history. Two of his decisions changed the course of events: the first was his adoption of Christianity and the other his foundation of Constantinople. He was born, out of wedlock, at Niš, and rose by his military gifts; he never lost a battle throughout his career. His father had become the Augustus in the west, but died in distant Britain a year after Diocletian's retirement. Constantine was proclaimed Emperor by his troops at York, but he had to fight his path to power from this remote cantonment. Near Rome in 312 he defeated Maxentius, his principal rival in the west. It was before this battle that Constantine traditionally had a vision of the cross in the sky, with the words 'Conquer by this.' He now came to an agreement with the eastern Emperor, Licinius, and in 313, by the 'Edict of Milan' tolerance was extended to Christianity. From being an underground cult, which had recently been savagely persecuted, the followers of Christ moved rapidly into a privileged position and an alliance with the secular powers. The change was momentous both for the Church and for the Empire. Licinius remained a pagan, and relations between the two deteriorated. In 323 Constantine marched eastwards, and in two decisive battles annihilated his rival. The second was fought at sea off Chrysopolis (Scutari) on the Asiatic side of the Bosporos, in September 324.

Constantine was now supreme ruler of the Roman world, and he must already have resolved to fix the position of the eastern capital. Legend credits him with various options – his birthplace at Naissus (Niš), Sardica (the Sofia of today), a site near Troy, and Chalcedon. Byzantium had been loyal to Licinius and Constantine had besieged and taken it. Like Severus a century before, he had begun by damaging the existing walls; but his soldier's eye had also perceived the strategic value of the city. It is not necessary to believe that a symbolic flight of two eagles eventually distracted his attention from Chalcedon.

The decision appears to have been taken towards the end of 324 and work began at once. Progress was so rapid that the new capital was formally dedicated on 11 May, 330. By the time of Constantine's death in 337, the new city was probably almost complete. It is believed that he intended it to be called 'Second Rome', but from the beginning the title of Constantinople – that is 'City of Constantine' – prevailed; and as prosperity developed here, the original Rome shrank into decay.

Before we examine the new metropolis, one or two other features of Constantine's reign deserve attention. He was successful (where Diocletian had failed) in stabilizing the currency. This was done on a gold basis; the unit was first known as a *Fig. 2* 'solidus', later as a 'nomisma' and from the thirteenth century as a 'hyperperos'; to the western world it was simply and grandly a bezant, and gave its name to the gold disc of heraldry. The solidus weighed about $4\frac{1}{2}$ grams (a sovereign weighs almost 8 grams) and remained undebased until the middle of the eleventh century; few coins have shown such staying power, and even after this date it still retained a high international reputation. Supported by lesser coins in silver and bronze, this robust, generally beautiful, and enduring coinage was a contributory factor to the economic growth of Constantinople.

THE CHURCH   The great Emperor had to take seriously his role as the patron of Christianity. The new position of the Church made clear, and made public, that there were grave divergences in doctrine. Soon after his triumph in Italy he had been confronted with the implications of the Donatist heresy, and had endorsed the findings of the Council of Arles. Now, as the lustrous buildings of Constantinople arose, he was faced with the Arian heresy and its numerous followers. This is no place to dig into the foundations of theology. Arius was a priest of Alexandria, too monotheist to accept the full divinity of Christ. In 325 Constantine summoned a council at Nicaea to seek unity: it was the first of the Oecumenical Councils of the Church, and he took a full share in the proceedings, thus indicating a facet of the imperial position which his successors were to develop. The council was attended by many more bishops from the east than from the west, but then the great Christological heresies were themselves an eastern rather than a western problem. Arianism was condemned and the Emperor exulted that 'the devil will no longer have any power against us'. His hopes were not to be fulfilled, but the council constituted a milestone in the relations of Church and State and in the development of a detailed creed.

At about the same time, his mother, St Helen, journeyed to Jerusalem and conducted a series of excavations. Her spade was richly rewarded; the True Cross was unearthed and most of the relics of the Passion discovered. In later centuries the repute of Constantinople as a guardian of sacred objects was to be unequalled; it is probably true to say that none of the great relics of the Church, and few of its holy places, have a warranted history which extends behind the activity of the Emperor's mother. This is not to doubt their authenticity, but the circumstances of the Church before 313 were not conducive to the preservation of records other than by word of mouth. Constantine himself was not baptized until he lay dying in 337, and even then the rite was administered by a bishop of Arian sympathies. Late baptism was not unusual in this period, but even so the nature of the Emperor's affiliation to Christianity has been hotly debated. To some he has seemed a politician, who embraced a faith offering practical advantages; to others his conversion is but another example of the shift of emphasis from the troubled west to the more prosperous, albeit more theological, eastern half of the Empire; to later divines he became a numinous figure, the second founder of Christendom, *Isapostolos*, the equal of, or even the thirteenth of the Apostles. The historian must pick his doubtful track between inadequate signposts. On the mundane side, the career of Constantine exhibited strange brutalities, such as the mysterious murder of his wife and son; spiritually, he was fully conscious of his duties towards the religious body he had selected for patronage. But of one material achievement there seems to be no doubt. The choice of Byzantium, and the care lavished on the chosen site, were responsible for one of the great deliberate urban centres of the world. If legendary founders may be ignored, the creation of Alexandria or St Petersburg are those which leap to comparison. Failed cities – Ur, Angkor, Chichen Itzá, Fatehpur Sikri – litter the globe. Constantine, then, may not have been a conventional Christian hero, but he was a resolute ruler, a soldier of uncommon skill and a man whose decisions were epoch-making and were firmly carried into effect. By his act Christian Europe was established and by his city it was to be preserved in its moment of greatest danger. The Gods of Olympus, their lustre already dimmed, began their sad descent to the ruined site and the museum corridor.

NEW ROME   Numismatic evidence suggests that the first intention of Constantine may have been merely to rehabilitate Byzantium and give it his name. But his relations with old Rome took a turn for the worse in 325, and by the solemn consecration in 330 Constantinople was emphatically the capital of the east and a rival to the city on the Tiber. No effort or expense was spared in this enterprise. The site of Severan Byzantium was greatly enlarged. According to a fifth-century historian (Philostorgius)

see Fig. 3

the Emperor traced the line of his walls himself with his spear, and when his companions were amazed at their extent, Constantine replied: 'I shall keep on until He who walks ahead of me will stop.' No trace of his ramparts remains today, but their course is known; it followed an arc rather more than a mile inside the present walls. Within them were all the appurtenances of a capital which could rival Rome, a Senate House, a Capitol, a main forum, a mile-post from which all distances were measured. When the expansion took place, Constantinople also boasted seven hills and fourteen districts, as did old Rome. The new capital had, therefore, a threefold destiny. By history it was linked to Rome and the Empire, by foundation it was a great Christian centre, by situation and language it was Greek and tied to the Hellenistic world of Alexander the Great and to the intellectual heritage of classical Greece. It should be added that for some time the emperors continued to be peripatetic, and it was not until towards the end of the century that they resided regularly at Constantinople.

The plan laid out by Constantine was definitive; it formed the centre of the city for the rest of its history. It is perhaps easiest to describe with reference to the existing church of Hagia Sophia (not of course then built). A short distance from the south-west corner was the Milion, from which all roads were measured. It appears to have been a cupola sustained by four triumphal arches; at the summit Constantine and St Helena displayed the cross. South-westwards from the Milion ran the length of the Hippodrome, with its curved end (the Sphendone) borne on arches to counteract the slope of the hill. South-east of the Milion was a group of official buildings and behind them the complex of the imperial palace. Directly westward from the Milion ran a broad street already laid out by Severus. But where the west gate had stood in the Severan wall, Constantine laid out a great forum. It was oval in shape and in the centre stood a towering column of porphyry. Later writers asserted that at the

Plate 2

23

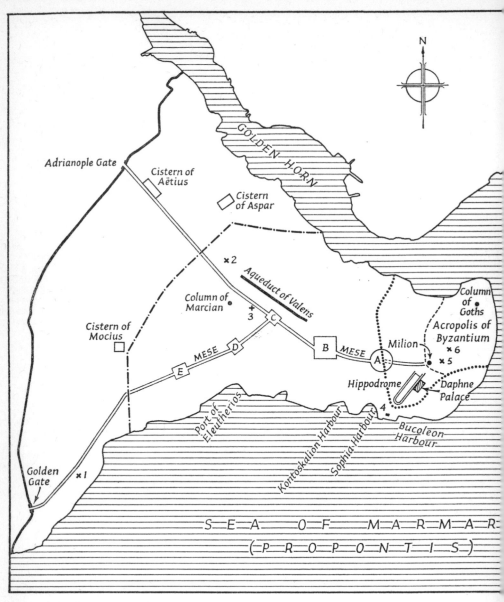

Fig. 3   The Constantinian and Severan city

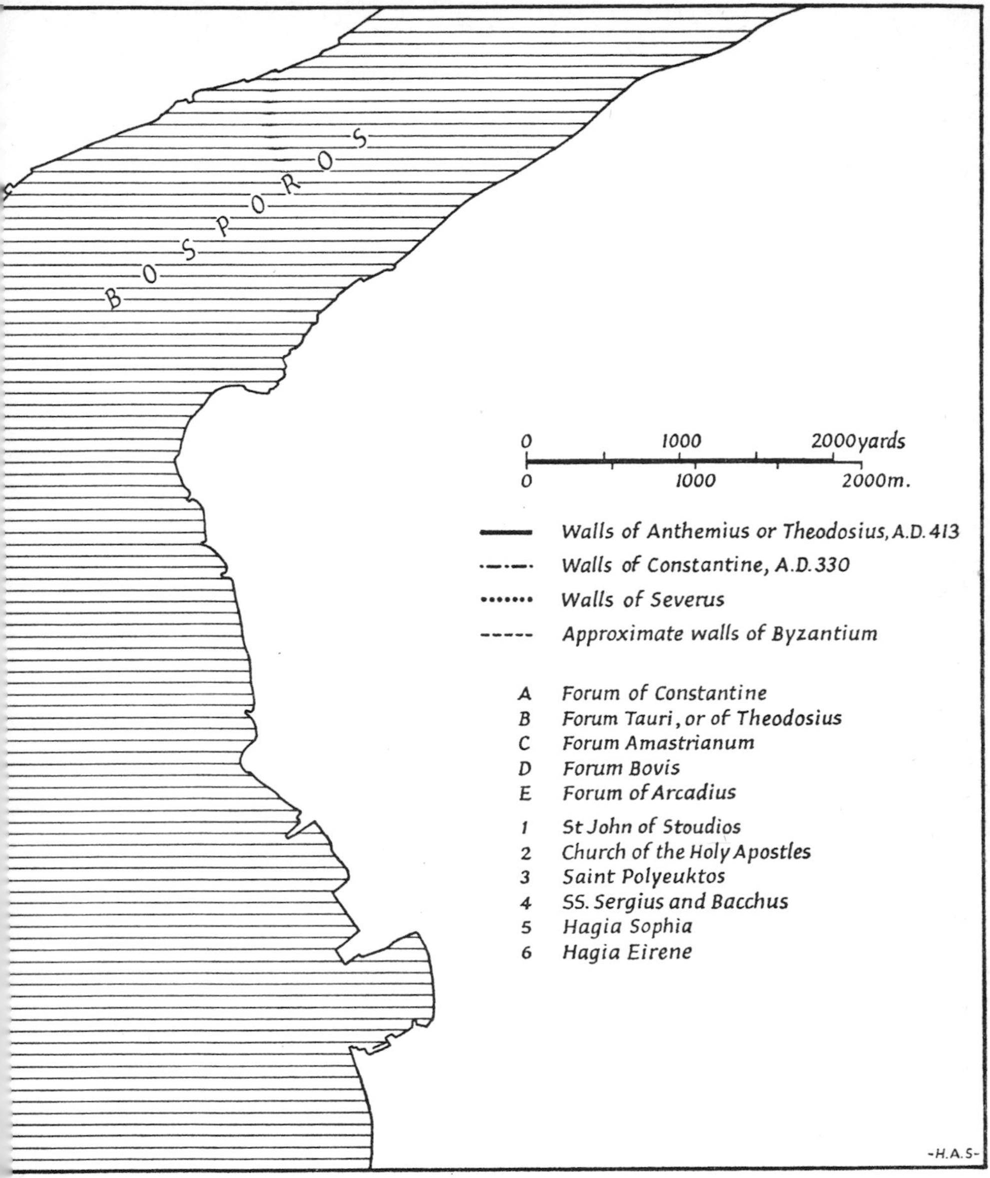

B-O-S-P-O-R-O-S

0	1000	2000 yards
0	1000	2000 m.

———— Walls of Anthemius or Theodosius, A.D. 413

—·—·— Walls of Constantine, A.D. 330

········ Walls of Severus

------ Approximate walls of Byzantium

A   Forum of Constantine
B   Forum Tauri, or of Theodosius
C   Forum Amastrianum
D   Forum Bovis
E   Forum of Arcadius

1   St John of Stoudios
2   Church of the Holy Apostles
3   Saint Polyeuktos
4   SS. Sergius and Bacchus
5   Hagia Sophia
6   Hagia Eirene

-H.A.S-

25

base of this imposing monument were deposited not only Christian relics, the crosses of the two thieves, the alabaster jar of St Mary Magdalene and the baskets of the miraculous loaves, but also the palladium of ancient Rome, the wooden statue of Athene brought by Aeneas from Troy. This last may be a conscious effort to attach Constantinople to the Trojan Legend but it illustrates the importance with which this column and forum were regarded. On the summit stood a statue of the Emperor, vested as Apollo. His family had cherished the cult of Sol Invictus (whose feast has been borrowed for the modern Christmas Day), and there was an element of the traditional in this portrayal; none the less the orb carried by the figure contained a fragment of the True Cross. The column itself was fashioned of nine great drums, and the original level of the forum lay some 16 feet below the present ground. The statue and the three upper drums were blown down by a mighty gale in 1105. Further damage was done by fire at different times and in 1701 the Sultan Mustafa III encircled it with the present iron rings (originally wreaths of bronze) and reinforced the lower part with a stone support. The present Turkish name (Çemberlitaş) means Burned Column. All around the forum were a profusion of statues and monuments, and a number of churches, mostly no doubt small. As the traveller approached it, he passed on the left the Martyrion of St Euphemia and on the right the Basilica. He entered through two great arches of white marble. Beyond the forum, the road turned slightly to the northwest and after a while forked, the northern arm going towards Adrianople and the southern towards Thessalonica.

The other notable piece of Constantine's handiwork is the Delphic Column in the Hippodrome. Erected at the shrine of Apollo by the victors of Plataea in 478 BC, it was originally composed of three entwined serpents on whose heads rested a golden tripod. The tripod disappeared long before Constantine moved the trophy from Delphi. Today even the heads are gone

Fig. 4   Constantine presenting the city. Mosaic at entrance to Hagia Sophia. About AD 990

(though a large fragment of one is in the Archaeological Museum). By some accounts Michael III (842–67) broke off the heads, but all three are clearly shown in a manuscript in the Saray Library describing the circumcision of one of the sons of Sultan Murat III (1582); one illustration at least (folio 308b) distinctly shows one of the heads lacking a lower jaw. Several travellers report them at the beginning of the seventeenth century; they were probably destroyed soon after this.

Fig. 5

It is likely that there was already a small church on the site of Hagia Eirene, and that Constantine rebuilt it on a larger scale and gave it the dedication of Holy Peace. It is less clear whether he, or his son Constantius, actually began the neighbouring church of Holy Wisdom (Santa Sophia: Hagia Sophia) which was solemnly consecrated in February, 360. In any case both were destroyed in the Nika riots of 532. No ecclesiastical build, ing of the age of the founder survives, though he was lavish in constructing them.

By 363 the house of Constantine was extinct; its last ruler had been Julian the Apostate who sought in vain to re-establish paganism during his brief reign (361–3). He constructed a small harbour, now vanished, a little to the west of SS. Sergius and Bacchus. In 364 the eastern throne was held by the Em, peror Valens who constructed the great aqueduct which bears his name and which still bestrides the valley between the third and fourth hills, giving passage in the twentieth century to the traffic of the Atatürk Boulevard. This majestic work was begun in 368, using stones from the walls of Chalcedon, which had been in rebellion. It has frequently needed restoration, and in fact ten of the arches (nos. 41–5 and 52–6 from the western end) are almost entirely the work of Sultans Mustafa II and Süleyman the Magnificent respectively. The water was carried to a large reservoir, the Nymphaeum Majus, roughly on the site of the modern University. Until a fire in 1907 the aqueduct was largely hidden by houses; it still carries water.

Plate 3

The aqueduct is a memorial to Valens, but his reign ended in disaster. For many years the onslaughts of the barbarians on the northern frontier of the empire had been waxing in strength. Peace had been achieved with Persia on the eastern frontier, but the Danube was under constant pressure. In 378 Valens was overwhelmed and slain at Adrianople by a force of Goths who had been driven southwards by the impulse of the Huns behind them. The situation was serious, and Gratian, the Emperor in

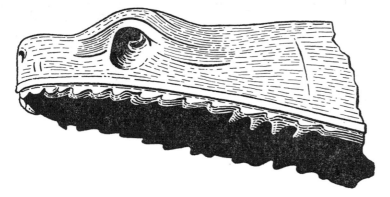

Fig. 5   Head of Delphic serpent, now in the Archaeological Museum, Istanbul

the west, committed the east to the charge of Theodosius, a Spaniard, son of an earlier general who had achieved an outstanding work of reconstruction in Britain. The choice was notable. Theodosius and his family restored the Roman Empire in the east and transformed Constantinople.

THEODOSIUS I

Theodosius I (379–95) was an orthodox Christian – Valens had been an Arian – and installed as Patriarch the great saint and scholar, Gregory Nazianzen. In 381 the second Oecumenical Council of the Church was held at Constantinople; it met in the then church of Eirene. The beliefs of Arius ceased to be a serious problem in the east; and since all other cults were now proscribed, Christianity became completely the state religion. Gratian, who had nominated Theodosius, was the last emperor to hold the position of Pontifex Maximus (supreme priest) which he gave up in 379; the title had been held by every emperor since Augustus.

Within his capital the Emperor constructed a large forum, which bore his name but was also sometimes called the Forum Tauri. Its site is just west of the Mosque of Beyazıt, and it is a

nodal point in the communications of the city. In the centre
stood a great column, erected in 396, with spiral reliefs depicting
his military triumphs and manifestly an imitation of Trajan's
column in Rome. Originally it was crowned by a statue of
Theodosius in silver, but this was shaken down by an earthquake in 480. It was from the summit of this column that the
hapless Alexius IV was flung to his death in 1204. Finally it
was demolished by Sultan Beyazıt II in about 1500. Two fragments can still be seen in the bath which he erected near by, and
it is probable that other fragments are encased in its walls. On
one side of the forum was a triumphal arch the base of which
was uncovered in 1928. It is difficult to envisage its appearance,
for it seems to have been a breakaway from classical style. A
portion of one pillar is gripped by a giant hand, and others are
decorated with a highly individual pattern of peacock's feathers.
This arch was shaken down by earthquake in 740, and later a
Turkish Han, the central depot for the silversmiths, was built
on and round the site. An odder ornament of the forum was a
bronze group of insects – mosquito, gnat, flea and so on –
allegedly made by Apollonius of Tyana and devised to protect
the city from such pests. This was misguidedly destroyed by
Basil I.

Theodosius also added a trophy, which still stands, to the
Hippodrome. It is a gigantic obelisk of granite, which was
transported from Karnak in Egypt and which celebrates the
victories of Thutmose III who set it up in 1471 BC. Once
crowned by a bronze sphere, it still rests firmly on four bronze
cubes: beneath them is a most interesting carved base of the
date of Theodosius, a key monument in the transition from
classical to later sculpture. On the four faces are seen the Emper-
or presiding at the games from the royal box and presenting
wreaths, and other activities of the Hippodrome. The north
side shows the obelisk itself being drawn into position. The
figures portrayed face more to the front than was usual in tra-

Plate 6

Plate 5

Plate 7
Plates 4, 5

Plate 10

Plate 9

ditional carving and offer a prophecy of the later Byzantine style. Also of interest are the two inscriptions, one in Latin and one in Greek, which remind us of the bilingual character of the capital at this date. In the former, the name of the prefect Proclus has been chiselled out and restored: he was disgraced in 392 but rehabilitated four years later. Both inscriptions claim that the obelisk was erected in 32 days.

This obelisk, and also the Delphic serpent erected by Constantine, stand in pits which demonstrate how much the level of the ground has risen since the fourth century. It may be convenient to mention here the third surviving monument of the many which once stood on the 'spina', or central rib of the Hippodrome. It is another obelisk, in dressed stone, about 100 feet high. Nobody knows who erected it, but Constantine VII Porphyrogenitus (913–59) restored it in memory of his grandfather, Basil I. The whole was covered with bronze-gilt plates commemorating Basil's deeds, and the Greek inscription at the base compares it favourably with the Colossus of Rhodes. However, the plates were looted by the men of the Fourth Crusade and the obelisk is today somewhat uninteresting.

At the south end of the walls stands the splendid entrance known as the Golden Gate. This was probably also the work of Theodosius I. An inscription on the voussoirs of the central arch (which can still be read from the dowel-holes of the vanished letters) states that Theodosius made the Golden Gate 'post fata tyranni' – after the doom of the usurper. At first sight it would seem more logical to associate this magnificent portal with Theodosius II who, as will be seen, built the adjoining land walls, but he did not have to suppress any great revolt in his reign: his grandfather, on the other hand, put down the rising of Maximus in 388 and this is the generally accepted date and origin of the gate. The plan is simple and imposing: a large arch between two lesser entries is flanked on the west by two great marble pylons. In front of them is an outwork and a

Plate 8

deep moat. This was the assembly point for the great procession when an emperor returned in triumph to the city. Here came, for example, Heraclius after his recovery of the True Cross, or Basil II after his great slaughter of the Bulgars. Here many new emperors were first welcomed by the civic authorities. But the Golden Gate also witnessed frustrations: the ferocious Khan Krum of the Bulgars, unable to penetrate the defences, celebrat⁄ ed human sacrifices in front of it, and proceeded to sprinkle the barbarian forces with sea⁄water in which he had bathed his feet. Neither expedient profited him at all (813) and he had to retire baffled, if somewhat cleaner.

At different periods the Gate was decorated with statuary of various kinds – a statue of Theodosius I, four large bronze ele⁄ phants, and a great figure of Victory. Many of them fell in earthquakes, and none is to be seen today. The lower, and per⁄ haps rather unworthy, propylons to the west were adorned with bas⁄reliefs of classical subjects (*e.g.* the Labours of Hercules); four of these were almost bought in 1625 by Sir Thomas Roe, the English Ambassador, on behalf of the Earl of Arundel and the Duke of Buckingham. But when he came to remove them, the local populace objected, believing that the fortunes of the city were bound up with that of the statuary. If Roe had brought off his purchase, we might have them still; their later fate is un⁄

Plate 53

known. In Turkish times the Golden Gate became part of the fortress of Yedikule (Seven Towers). (*Cf.* p3.2.).

ARCADIUS

When Theodosius I died in 395, he was the ruler of the whole Roman Empire: he recognized however that the task was too much for one man, and bequeathed the east to his elder son Arcadius (395–408) and the west to Honorius, the younger. The great emperor realised that the eastern half was now the more important, as it was also the richer and the more populous. Never again were the two halves to be fully united under one ruler, though the concept of unity did not disappear and was indeed esteemed.

Arcadius was not a potent sovereign; his actions effected little, while his court attracted the censures, and eventually led to the exile, of St John Chrysostom (of the Golden Mouth), another of the fathers of the Byzantine Church. None the less, he added another forum to those which decorated the main street of Constantinople. This was the Mēsē, one of the great streets of the world. Starting at the Milion, it ran westwards to the Forum of Constantine, turned slightly north-west to the Forum Tauri (or of Theodosius) and continued in that direction till the parting of the ways between the great routes to Adrianople and to Thessalonica. At this juncture there was probably another open space, the Forum Amastrianum, though the textual evidence for it is scanty; the area had a bad reputation, for public executions took place in it and there was a minatory sculpture exhibiting two hands containing a standard measure which served as a warning to dishonest merchants. Turning westward the Mēsē now passed through the Forum Bovis, named after a vast bronze ox-head brought from Pergamum. Here Julian the Apostate martyred some Christians, here the body of Phocas was burned in 610, and here at a later date perished some victims of the iconoclasts. Today the area is approximately under the Turkish Aksaray.

Slightly west of the Ox-Forum (though still within the walls of Constantine) was the Forum of Arcadius. This was on a hill called Xerolophos, from which it was also named. Here in 404 the Emperor set up a tall column, though his statue was only added by his son in 421. Like most of the forums – except that of Constantine – it was probably rectangular, but virtually no archaeological research has taken place in this area. The statue was brought down by the earthquake of 740, and the greater part of the column was deliberately demolished by the Turks in 1711, to preserve the houses around. But the base is still discoverable behind a baker's shop almost opposite the mosque of Cerrahpaşa, wrapped in ivy and oblivion.

Arcadius was followed by his son Theodosius II (408-50),
then seven years old. The boy grew up to be more interested in
calligraphy than government, but happily he had an able en-
tourage to act in face of the difficulties of the eastern empire.
News from the west was grim. In 410 Rome fell to Alaric and
his Goths. An even more barbarian race, the Huns, were menacing Constantinople, whose population and wealth were
constantly increasing. Accordingly in 413 the regent Anthemius, who held the office of prefect, constructed a new series of
defences, a mile or so west of those of Constantine. These walls,
which are sometimes named for him, and sometimes for his
master, remained unbreached by any foe for one thousand and
forty years, a superb record for any piece of fortification. (The
crusaders of 1204 broke in across the Golden Horn.) The large
amount which yet survives makes it superfluous to trace their
course in detail; they still constitute a masterpiece of military
architecture and a spur to the historical imagination. For the
whole development of Christian Europe was sheltered and
protected by these ramparts.

The walls of Anthemius run for four and a half miles from
the Sea of Marmara, taking in the Golden Gate just north of it,
to the Golden Horn. At this end their original line has been
adjusted to the buildings of the later Blachernae Palace. They
are built of limestone blocks, divided at intervals by bands of
narrow bricks, five deep, the whole filled with concrete. Ninety-
six towers projected from the main wall (it is tempting to suppose that there may have been 100 before the reconstruction at
the northern end), of which over 70 are square and the rest
polygonal. This main wall was 30 feet high on the outside and
16 feet thick. In front of it was a broad ditch, revetted with
stone, some 60 feet wide and 50 feet from the wall. The main
military aim was to bring the attacker under deadly fire as he
sought to cross the moat; the artillery of the day – ballistae,
onagri, and so forth – was quite capable of doing this and

could discharge by torsion stone balls of 100 lb. or more. In the fifteenth century gunpowder made this great system obsoles/cent. Much controversy reigns over the moat: it has partitions which seem designed to hold water at varying levels; several travellers describe it as full, but no account of a siege mentions a wet moat. Indeed, in the summer the volume of water required would surely have been needed for the citizens within. Earth/quakes and neglect have taken their toll since 1453, but these Theodosian land walls are still one of the great monuments of all time.

The first earthquake came in 447 and was disastrous. Not only did the shocks continue from November to January, but 57 towers were shaken down, and this when the hideous hosts of Attila were not far away. The emergency was met with re/solution. In two months of frantic labour, in which all parties joined, the demes of the Greens and Blues (see page 43 *infra*) for once competing in friendly rivalry, the walls were restored under the direction of a Constantine, the Praetorian Prefect. Nor was this all. A new wall was built between the ditch and the main wall with 92 towers; this addition also provided an area for the movement of troops between the two walls. An in/scription on the Rhegion gate boasted that Constantine achiev/ed rebuilding in less than two months and '*Tam cito tam stabilem Pallas vix conderet arcem.*' Indeed Athene could hardly have done better; for ten centuries the forces of barbarism, Huns, Avars, Bulgars, Pechenegs, Russians, Crusaders, Turks, were to view these bulwarks and recoil.

Plate 12

There had already been walls on the sea/side of the cities of Severus and Constantine the Great. Under Theodosius II the circuit was completed to join the new land walls. This work was somewhat later and was associated with the Prefect Cyrus and the year 439. From the top of the Golden Horn to Saray point there was a simple wall, 30 feet high, with 110 towers and 14 gates; from Saray point to the Golden Gate were 188 towers

Plate 31 and at least a dozen openings. This last section was a good deal damaged when the railway was constructed in 1871.

Theodosius II also had religious problems: his reign witnessed the third great Church Council (at Ephesus in 431) which condemned the Nestorians and proclaimed that the Virgin was indeed 'Theotokos', Mother of God. He also made a great collection of laws – the Codex Theodosianus – in Latin, and refounded the University at Constantinople. The school was housed in a building called the Octagon; it was near the modern Basilican Cistern. Three orators and ten grammarians taught Latin, five orators and ten grammarians taught Greek – an interesting indication of the growing importance of the latter; there were also a chair of philosophy and two of law. A more material innovation, engineered by the Prefect Cyrus, was the lighting of the streets by night.

The successors of Theodosius were less active, but the city continued to thrive, and some striking private benefactions still survive.

In honour of the Emperor Marcian (450–7) a column was erected; its Turkish name (Kıztaşı = young lady's pillar) alludes to the carved Victories on the base. Great open-air cisterns were constructed in various parts of the city. Of these, the one associated with the name of Aëtius can easily be seen near the Adrianople Gate; today it houses an entire football pitch. It dates from 421 and was already dry in the sixteenth century. The Alan general Aspar constructed another (near the Mosque of Sultan Selim), while the biggest of all, that of St Mocius, was associated with the monastery of that name, just west of the Constantinian wall. It measures 170 metres by 147.

ST JOHN OF
STOUDIOS
One very important church survives from this century, that belonging to the great monastery of St John of Stoudios, important not only in its own right as one of the great theological centres of the capital, but also as the only large church prior to

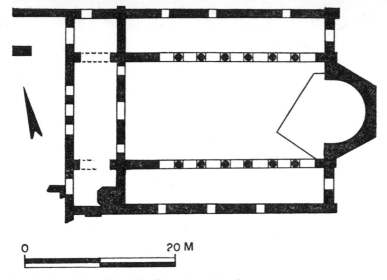

Fig. 6   Ground plan of St John of Stoudios. AD 463

Fig. 6

the age of Justinian. On its ruins must be based our ideas of the
multitude of other churches which we know to have existed.
This house of religion was established in 463 by the Patrician
Stoudios, consul for the east in 454. Its monks were known as
the Sleepless Ones, because they celebrated the divine liturgy in
relays without cease. In the eighth and ninth centuries it was a
powerful centre of resistance to the Iconoclast doctrines. Three
later patriarchs came hence; its rites were used in the establishment of Mount Athos in the tenth century. Three Byzantine
emperors, fallen from state, took their vows here. Every living
emperor came hither, by sea, on the feast of the beheading of the
Baptist (29 August), whose head was the most precious relic
of the monastery.

    In Roman times a basilica was an official hall sometimes
with aisles and normally with a semicircular apse at one end;
the name was really functional more than stylistic, and the
building could serve as law-court, market or even riding-school.

Fig. 7   St John of Stoudios, before 1894

There was a large basilica just west of the Milion in Constantinople. When the Christian Church became established and
needed large places of worship, this type of building commend-
ed itself, as it had done to other cults. One of the great achievements of Byzantine architecture was to turn the basilican form
into something new, but the church of St John represents an
orthodox use of the form. The nave is divided from the aisles by
two rows of columns of which only the northern stand today.
Formerly there were galleries in the aisles and at the west end,
carried on richly carved entablatures. In its heyday, the walls of
the church were lined with marble; it was however plundered
by the crusaders in 1204, damaged by earthquake in 1894, and
again by fire in 1920. The elaborate paving dates from the
restoration of the church in 1290 or so, to repair the crusaders'
damage. The apse has a polygonal exterior, and a small cruciform crypt, both breaks with tradition; there is a cistern on the

Fig. 7

Plate 15

Plates 16, 17

south side. It was turned into a mosque (Imrahor Ilyas bey camii) in about 1500 by the Master of Horse to Beyazıt II; the floor still bears evidence of the consequent alterations at the east end. Today the basilica of St John stands silent and empty (and not always easy of access) but whispers of the wealth of church‑building which adorned the early city. At different dates there were 35 distinct churches in the capital dedicated to the Baptist, but this was always the most important.

Fig. 8

In 753 BC the city of Rome, according to legend, was found‑ed by Romulus, the she‑wolf's suckling. On the last day of Oc‑tober, AD 475, the Patrician Orestes advanced to the imperial dignity his own little son, Romulus Augustulus, diminutive alike in reign and title: the elevation was not recognized in Constantinople. Next year, the barbarian forces in Italy depos‑ed Romulus and chose a Teutonic chief, Odoacer; in 480 the exiled western Emperor Julius Nepos died in Dalmatia. These dates have been clutched at as marking the end of the empire in the west; to accept this is to misunderstand the situation. Since

Fig. 8   Narthex of St John of Stoudios, before 1894

39

the era of Diocletian there had been sometimes one, and some-times two, emperors, but they were a team. In Constantinople, Zeno (not without difficulty) continued to reign, and the Em-pire founded by Augustus did not terminate until the Ottoman Turks broke through the walls in 1453. Then, and then only, did the decline of the Roman Empire end in fall, and that fall was the fall of Constantinople.

In the meantime, the city stood strong behind the fifth-century walls. And yet between 507 and 512 the Emperor Ana-stasius (491–518) constructed a rampart 40 miles inland from the city to join the Black Sea and the Marmara with an outer girdle of defence, some 41 miles in length. The work consisted of a stout stone wall with towers. It is noteworthy that the modern Turkish Çatalca lines, which may have contributed to German reluctance to invade Turkey in the last war, followed approximately the same course. However, the wall of Ana-stasius did not prevent subsequent invaders reaching the im-perial city itself.

Excavations in 1960 revealed traces of an important church, dedicated to St Polyeuktos, near the modern town hall of Istanbul. This was built in AD 524–7 by Anicia Juliana, a cadet of the family of Theodosius. The ground plan still has to be elucidated fully, but a capital was unearthed which is iden-tical with two well-known ones on free-standing piers outside St Mark's at Venice. These have hitherto been supposed to come from Acre; but the possibility must exist that they came from St Polyeuktos, which had fallen into decay by the time of the Fourth Crusade in 1204.

Fig. 1

Plate 14

CHAPTER III

The Age of Justinian

> This then the city by the wide world desired
> Which seized the royal garland of the globe
> Which grasped the sceptre and the crown of Rome
>
> CONSTANTINE THE RHODIAN I.59-61

THERE HAS BEEN MUCH DISPUTE among scholars as to when the Byzantine age really begins, or that of late Rome ends. It is indeed curious that we use the adjective drawn from Byzantium to describe the art and civilization of Constantinople – but no odder than applying the term 'Gothic' to the pointed architecture of the thirteenth century. There is much to be said for the view that the reign of Justinian (527–65) left the capital, and perhaps the Empire also, so changed that thenceforward they had a new character of their own. This is above all true of architecture, but there are more general factors which must be considered.

Fig. 9

We have seen how Diocletian initiated the division of the Roman Empire into two spheres of west and east, while never denying the fundamental unity. We have seen furthermore that in the fifth century the structure of the western half crumbled under barbarian assaults. It was the ambition of Justinian to re-establish the unity and to rule once more over the whole Mediterranean world. By the brilliance of his generals – especially Belisarius and Narses – and by a lavish expenditure of men and money, he came within measurable distance of accomplishing his ends; in fact the resources of the east were not sufficient for this gigantic task. The price of Justinian's endeavour was fiscal oppression and the collapse of his other hopes of financial and social reform. He was also compelled to pay insufficient attention to his eastern frontiers. But no later emperor was able to attempt the reunion of the lands round the central sea; hence-

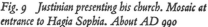
Fig. 9   Justinian presenting his church. Mosaic at entrance to Hagia Sophia. About AD 990

forward the destinies of east and west, though linked in many ways, were to be politically discrete.

In religious matters too he faced a dilemma. His preoccupations with Italy demanded good relations with Rome and an orthodox faith, but large numbers of Christians in Syria and Egypt were increasingly attracted by monophysite views (the idea that Jesus Christ had only one nature, not two). These tenets had been condemned at the Council of Chalcedon in 451, along with those of the Nestorians. In 553 he held the fifth general Council at Constantinople and condemned the writing of three Nestorian divines, but this exercise failed to win much gratitude from the monophysites, who counted Justinian's own wife among their supporters. Discontent in Syria and Egypt undoubtedly contributed to the rapid advance of Islam in the next century.

In ordinary life Justinian is perhaps most remembered for his great codification of Roman Law. The Corpus Juris Civilis continued to be a standard book in the east, but did not make its way into western Europe until the twelfth century. It was written in Latin, but the additions made to it later in his reign, called Novels (new laws), are almost all in Greek. In Novel 7 Justinian declared, 'We have written this decree not in the native language, but in the spoken Greek in order that it may become known to all.' The process was a slow one, not accomplished in a single generation; but here is a milestone in the replacement of Latin by Greek as the official, as well as the spoken, tongue of the Empire. There was in fact a spate of Greek commentaries on the work done in Latin.

Justinian was by any standards a great builder, and his handiwork can be found from Ravenna to Mount Sinai. But the internal politics of the capital gave him a special opportunity in Constantinople itself, of which he made the most. Contestants and parties were required for the games in the Hippodrome, whether at Rome, Constantinople or other great cities. These were represented by the Greens and the Blues, organized in bodies called demes. There had been also Whites and Reds, but the two first-named outstripped them except for actual games. They were more than sporting corporations, however; they had civic and military responsibilities and could develop political and religious bias. We have already noticed their strenuous efforts on the walls in 447. To draw a broad comparison, it is rather as though the two great Glasgow football teams, Celtic and Rangers, added a note of civic duty and militia obligations

43

to their existing rivalries. If the palace was the seat of the Emperor, and the churches were the concern of the Patriarch, it was to the people, and to the two factions, that the Hippodrome belonged. Here emperors were made or unmade; here executions took place; here triumphs finished; here, and constantly, games and public spectacles were held. This vast space was about 400 yards long by 70 wide; there were 30–40 tiers of seats and accommodation for 100,000 people. By the time of Justinian, the Greens tended to favour the lower social orders and commerce and to encourage monophysitism, while the Blues had links with the senatorial aristocracy and orthodoxy. Anastasius, himself a monophysite, had been pro-Green; Justinian in youth was a Blue. But once on the throne he tried to bring both factions to order. In 532 the Greens and the Blues united in riot. Much of Constantinople was in flames; an obscure nephew of Anastasius was proclaimed Emperor; and Justinian, penned in his palace, contemplated flight. The early history of the Empress Theodora may have been doubtful, even if we do not believe all the wilder anecdotes of Procopius, but her heart was robust and her spirit high: 'I approve', she cried, 'of the old saying that the purple is a fair shroud.' Braver counsels prevailed and the disciplined soldiers of Belisarius put the rabble to rout. The Emperor's reign was saved, but much of the centre of his capital, including the great churches by the palace, was in ashes. The outbreak is usually called the 'Nika' riot, from the cry of 'Conquer!' which was yelled – in Greek of course – by the mob.

Justinian had begun his building operations before the 'Nika' riot. During his uncle's lifetime he occupied the Palace of Hormisdas, named after a Persian prince. Close to it, on the sea, stood another palace, linked with Leon Macellus, of which some vestiges still existed a century ago but have now disappeared. Near by an elegant façade, incorporated in the sea-wall, is

Fig. 10

Fig. 10 Vanished palace, as it appeared at the end of the nineteenth century. These remains might have been part of the palace of Leon Macellus

known as the 'House of Justinian', and is sometimes associated with the Palace of Hormisdas, which was in fact inland. This is actually a remnant of the Palace of Bucoleon, overlooking the little harbour of that name, which provided an important entry from the sea. Today we can see three great windows with traces of a balcony in front: behind them is a vaulted chamber, partly resting on an earlier sea-wall. The modern motor road conceals the fact that these windows once looked directly over the Propontis, and that boats could probably sail into the blocked archway on the left, whence a stair led up into the main palace on a higher level. The loggia we now behold, though constructed of earlier materials, may possibly belong to the eighth century.

Saint Sergius and Saint Bacchus were two relatively obscure saints, Roman officers martyred under Maximian, but Justinian believed himself to be in their debt for an intercession with Anastasius. Accordingly, he built a most remarkable church in their honour. At that time the site was an exceedingly constricted

Plate 18
Figs. 11, 12

Plate 19

SS. SERGIUS
AND
BACCHUS

45

Fig. 11   Reconstruction of Bucoleon Palace (possibly eighth century AD) and the harbour

Fig. 13

one. There was already a church of SS. Peter and Paul, apparently immediately to the south, and of a basilican form,
while the east was probably hemmed in by the fabric of the
Palace. The new church was not however basilican in shape;
it takes the form of an inner octagon with a central dome, encased on all sides (except the east) with aisles and galleries. The
design is virtually a prototype for the far vaster church of Hagia
Sophia; but since SS. Sergius and Bacchus was constructed between 527 and 536, the design must have been well advanced
before the need to reconstruct Hagia Sophia arose after the
'Nika' riot in 532. The architects of this smaller church are unknown; their work has some technical imperfections in the way
of symmetry (possibly from the extreme constriction of the site),
but the whole effect is one of considerable beauty. This might
be even more striking if the level of the floor had not been raised
at various dates, and if the whole character had not been changed by conversion into a mosque in about 1500 by the chief of
the White Eunuchs.

If the design and plan of the building were forward-looking,
they were not revolutionary. Domed buildings were not un-

known, and there had been many shrines based on a four-lobed plan. In Ravenna, and at almost exactly the same time, the architects of the Emperor were constructing San Vitale, but here the exterior as well as the interior was eight-sided. Though it is tempting to imagine links between the two, the exercise is almost certainly fruitless. The internal decoration of SS. Sergius and Bacchus also marked a step forward; it was on a lavish scale. Procopius tells us that it and its neighbour of SS. Peter and Paul (of which no trace whatsoever remains, though the two appear to have had a common porch) outshone the sun by the gleam of their masonry and were rich with quantities of gold. Today the glittering marbles have largely disappeared, and it is easier to admire the heavily undercut capitals and the replacement of classical foliage by spiky acanthus motifs which are assuredly Byzantine in quality and technique. A feature of the decoration is a bold frieze in Greek lettering which runs round the interior octagon, below the galleries, and honours the memory of Justinian, of Theodora and of Saint Sergius.

Fig. 12   Interior of Bucoleon Palace, looking east. Through this arch, no longer standing, could be seen the hills of Asia

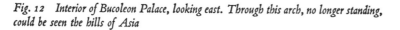

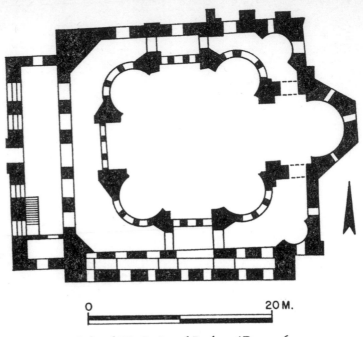

Fig. 13   Ground plan of SS. Sergius and Bacchus. AD 527–36

The ground plan is simple, but effective. Eight substantial piers sustain the dome and are divided at the entrance and to right and left by pairs of pillars. In the four corners, similar pillars also, of green and red marble, are set back to form exedrae (large recessed niches). Some critics have expressed doubts on the success of this interior, but the general lines are surely pleasing; and the contrasts between the straight and curving lines are successful as they stand and prophetic of glories to come. When the church became a mosque in about 1500, the existing arcade with five cupolas was added to the western façade. A later minaret, whose base can still be seen, was destroyed in 1937. By a pleasing and perceptive turn of phrase, the Turks call it 'Küçük Ayasofya Camii' or 'Little Hagia Sophia.'

The most noble of the churches of Justinian is next in date, the reconstructed fane of Hagia Sophia, the unquestioned and unquestionable masterpiece of this age. It is convenient to view first its neighbour, the church of Hagia Eirene (or Irene). In the case of both it cannot be stated too clearly that their dedications are not to female saints, but to attributes of the Supreme Godhead. Hagia Sophia represents the Divine Wisdom, and Hagia Eirene the Divine Peace of Almighty God; neither commemorates fallible humanity.

Both had prior buildings on the site: both were destroyed in the 'Nika' riots. The site of Eirene may have been the earlier; there may even have been a pagan temple of Peace here before a primitive Christian sanctuary which in turn was reconstructed by Constantine. After the dedication of the new Hagia Sophia in 360, the two churches were regarded as a pair within one sacred enclosure. In Hagia Eirene was probably held the Council of Constantinople in 381. From 404 to 415 it served as cathedral when Hagia Sophia had been damaged by fire.

HAGIA EIRENE

Eirene was rebuilt by Justinian after 532, but with less emphasis and splendour than the next-door church. And in any case the new church was badly damaged again by fire in 564, and by an earthquake in 738. The present shape was only achieved by degrees through these several reconstructions. It must be assumed that any church before the time of Justinian was simply basilican in form; that Emperor and his successors modified the basilica into a new concept. Justinian imposed a dome over the eastern end of the original ground plan; an apse remained at the east end (though with a polygonal exterior, reminiscent of that at Stoudios); thus the area to the west of the high altar was crowned by a large dome supported on four substantial piers. The sense of an aular plan was preserved by four columns on each side making an arcade between the piers. The effect of this today has been somewhat spoiled by the replacement by the Turks of the original, no doubt matching, pillars with a mixed

Plate 20

Fig. 14

Plate 21

collection of substitutes of unequal size. The transeptal sense provided by these arcades was probably emphasized in the reconstruction of 564; we have therefore the elements of a cruciform, domed church replacing the simpler and traditional basilican plan of a rectangle with an eastern apse. The semicircular seats for the clergy at the east end probably date from the eighth-century rebuilding. The west end of the nave was covered by a lateral barrel vault, later replaced by a low dome. Eirene is a transitional church; if one surveys it from the extreme west end – where the atrium, or forecourt, is unusually well preserved – one might almost be looking along a conventional basilica to the apse; but to stand under the dome is to envisage the cruciform church of later centuries stretching out its four arms from under a cupola. The conch of the apse is decorated with a fine cross in mosaic, dating presumably from Justinian, and traces of an early pavement have been discovered under the present floor.

The later fate of Hagia Eirene was unusual. It was not turned into a mosque at any time, but became a museum or arsenal of artillery. Even today its surroundings are freely adorned with trophies of the gunner, drawn from various ages and realms; here, captured pieces boast the winged lion of St Mark side by side with the culverins or falconets wrought by Turkish artificers.

HOLY
APOSTLES

One great church of Justinian has perished altogether; it was that of the Holy Apostles where in due course he was to be interred. On the high spur of land which constitutes the fourth hill, and just within his walls, Constantine had begun in 336 a shrine to the Holy Apostles. The edifice was completed by his son and was consecrated in about 356; it contained the relics of St Timothy, St Luke and St Andrew. Later piety associated the sanctuary with St Helen, but she died some years before it was begun. Two hundred years of existence produced signs of wear and tear, and Justinian resolved on a completely new building; and the replacement was consecrated in 550. Constantine's martyrion had been cruciform; under a central drum

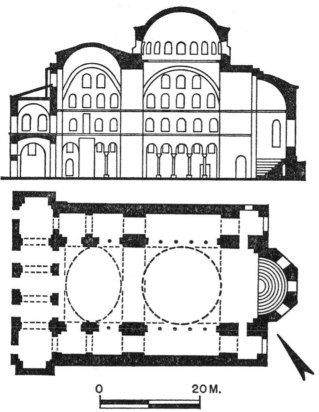

*Fig. 14 Ground plan and elevation of Hagia Eirene.
Mid eighth century AD*

and cone was the sarcophagus of the first Christian Emperor
himself, surrounded by the shrines of the apostles; a generation
later his body was removed from this too central position to a
separate mausoleum; the emphasis on the thirteenth apostle had
been too strong. Justinian followed the cruciform pattern, but
with a difference. His church was surmounted by five domes,
one central and one over each arm of the cross; there seems to
have been no apse and the altar was placed centrally. This great

cf. Plate 32

shrine became the established burial place for the Byzantine emperors, a parallel to St Denis or Westminster Abbey. Hither, after the macabre ritual of the funeral, came the cadaver of an emperor to rest with his predecessors in one of the great porphyry sarcophagi. These venerable tombs were ruthlessly looted by the men of the Fourth Crusade, and thereafter the rulers of the city tended to seek sepulture elsewhere. By the time of the Turkish conquest the church was in poor repair. For a year or two it was the seat of the Patriarch and then in 1461 Mehmet II ordered its destruction and used the site for the great mosque of the conqueror (Fatih) which was to immortalize his own memory. It was designed by the architect Sinan Atik and owed nothing to Byzantine influence. In 1766 an earthquake brought it down in ruins. The reigning Sultan, Mustafa III, erected another mosque on the same commanding site, which still dominates that quarter of Istanbul, but it was built at an unhappy period. The exterior has certain traditional qualities of mass, but within the uneasy impact of western idiom is already evident.

But the ghost of the Holy Apostles still stirs. The ground plan of St Mark's at Venice is a more or less direct reproduction of the Byzantine church and gives an impression, albeit a distorted one, of the appearance of Justinian's interior. The basic pattern, though with an extended nave, is also to be seen in the ruined, though partially reconstructed, church of St John the Evangelist, on a hill at Selçuk, a mile or so from the ancient Ephesus.

HAGIA
SOPHIA

Justinian's other buildings pale beside the splendour of his achievement in the church of the Holy Wisdom. It would appear that the earlier church on the site was completely destroyed in the 'Nika' riot (11–18 January, 532), and the Emperor acted quickly. Intending to create a new cathedral on an unsurpassed scale, he bought up property adjacent to the cindery remains and set his architects to work. Reconstruction began on 23 February and the entire masterpiece was completed within six years and dedicated on 27 December, 537. Through many vicissitudes, and despite some thirty major earthquakes and a number of menacing fires, the supernal shrine of the Holy Wisdom of God still stands on the rock where it was builded over 1400 years ago, a monument to the piety and resolution of the Emperor and the audacious skill of his architects.

Fig. 9

The latter were two Greeks from Asia Minor, Anthemius of Tralles and Isidore of Miletus. Anthemius was in truth more of a scientist than a builder or craftsman; a contemporary wrote that his skill was in the application of geometry to solid matter. Yet it is inconceivable that he was without previous experience: indeed the earlier church of SS. Sergius and Bacchus has been attributed to the same pair. It is also tempting to believe, though there is no evidence for the conjecture, that Emperor and architect already had in mind a gigantic church, and that the 'Nika' riot provided the opportunity and the site. If there was no premeditation, then the achievement of Anthemius and Isidore in a mere lustrum is all the more noteworthy. For they erected what is beyond dispute one of the truly great buildings of the world, and in the eyes of many the most noble and inspiring of all Christian churches.

No expense was spared; a host of labourers was assembled; the quarries of the Empire were searched for fine marbles. Translation of ancient totals into modern money is at best a hazardous essay; but it may be reckoned that a sum equivalent to at least £60,000,000 in current terms was dispensed. According to a late (tenth-century) source, Justinian cried out when he entered the completed building: 'O Solomon, I have surpassed thee.'

The design is basically simple, but aesthetically of extreme subtlety. Anthemius moved with mastery from his knowledge of geometry and optics to the control of mass and space; and

in order to achieve his effects he was prepared to take very substantial risks. Before describing his building, it has to be ad-
mitted that the great dome designed by him only lasted for a
score of years and had to be replaced by a different concept. In
favour of Anthemius we must remember that he was not only
required to produce a sensational edifice but to do so in a sen-
sationally short time.

Plate 22

The ground plan of the cathedral exhibits a rectangle 77 by
71 metres. But no internal observer is conscious of this square-
ness; he sees instead an enormous nave – really the historical
basilica – ending in an apse and crowned with a vast dome
which appears to float on air above him. To left and right he is
conscious of aisles and galleries, present but not emphasized;
the reality is the vast central, dome-crowned space, vaster than
anything built before or since in ecclesiastical architecture. For
example, the area of Hagia Sophia and St Paul's is almost iden-
tical; the dome of the latter is slightly higher (67 m. to 56), but
Wren's nave measures 13.41 m. across to the 31.0 of Hagia
Sophia which is wider also than the nave of St Peter's at Rome.

As one stands, then, at the west end of Hagia Sophia, having
passed through a considerable narthex, the traditional basilica
shape is covered by a central dome with two large half-domes to
west and east. This conceals the reality: the great central dome is
in fact based upon four robust, central piers and rests upon four
great arches poised upon them. The ingenuity of the architects
conceals the role of the north and south arches and converts
them at the lower levels into screens to emphasize the nave, and
above into a source of light. From the point of view of stress it
would have been more efficient to furnish two more half-domes
to north and south, but this would have entailed a cruciform
pattern alien to the intentions of Anthemius and Isidore. The
stark grandeur of the central, enclosed space is matched by the
elusive, and often mysterious glimpses of the aisles, and from
the aisles towards the middle. Indeed, at ground level the aisles

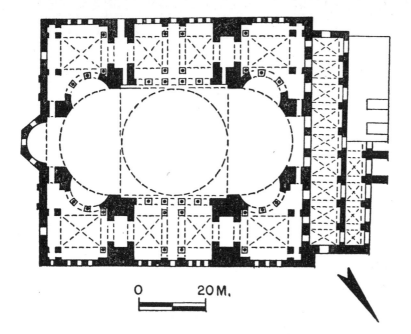

Fig. 15   Ground plan of Hagia Sophia AD 532-7

are so divided by buttresses as to constitute a series of three separate chambers rather than a continuous vista; this is perhaps
less so in the galleries.

Though the dome itself rests primarily on the four great
arches, the circle between them is translated into a square by
the four large pendentives, themselves a new and untried device
at this date. The dome has a diameter of 32 m. The existence of
the semi-domes to east and west prevents the main space being a
simple rectangle; the semi-domes are poised on four secondary
piers and between these and the four main piers are recessed,
curved openings called exedrae. In a sense, therefore, the plan
is loosely related to that of SS. Sergius and Bacchus but with
much greater emphasis on the central open space.

THE DOME

Plate 23

Fig. 15

55

As constructed by Anthemius, the dome was 6 m. lower than it is today and made a greater outwards thrust on the piers supporting it. Only the four main piers are built of solid masonry; the rest of the walls and supports are of bricks and mortar. The sixth-century technique of building used almost as much mortar as brick, a compound which can produce an exceedingly tough amalgam; in this case the speed of erection did not allow the mortar time to harden completely and considerable distortion of the walls was taking place before the dome was accomplished. Anthemius himself died, in 534, before the work was nearly finished. There was a bad earthquake in 553. By AD 557 the span of the dome at its base had spread by 5 feet. At the end of that year there was another serious earthquake, and on 7 May, 558, the eastern part of the dome collapsed and greatly damaged that end of the church. Restoration was confided to the younger Isidore, a nephew of the original Isidore of Miletus, and himself an accomplished architect. The work took five years and the cathedral was re-dedicated on 25 December, 563. Isidore deemed it essential to raise the height of the dome by 20 Byzantine feet (a Byzantine foot may be regarded as 0.315 metres) and he thus gave the dome the shape which it has maintained ever since. He furthermore strengthened the great arches to north and south by broadening their soffits and introducing more strength into the lunettes enclosed by them.

This was not the end of the story of the dome. In 986 the western arch collapsed: restoration under an Armenian architect, named Trdat, took until 994. In 1347, following another earthquake, the eastern arch again collapsed and took seven years to rebuild; the architects were Astras, Faciolatus and Giovanni Peralta, the last-named at least a Latin. In 1847 the dome was encircled with an iron chain by the Fossati brothers, acting under the orders of Sultan Abdul Mecid. Recent examination of the dome has shown that the 40 ribs can be divided among their authors; 13 at the east end are mainly the work of the restorers of 1347–54; five on the south and seven on the north belong to the first repair of the younger Isidore; the 15 at the west were wrought by Trdat. Of the three, the work of Isidore shows the highest craftsmanship.

The history of the dome has distracted us from the interior of Hagia Sophia. Originally the main approach was from an open courtyard, or atrium, to the west; nowadays the traveller enters from the south-west corner. The east range of the atrium formed an exonarthex, leading to a higher esonarthex, itself an enclosed space of considerable size and grandeur. Lavishness is the keynote of the internal decoration. We are well supplied with accounts of the original building; and they show that the sensational qualities of the edifice were appreciated from the start. It was, said Procopius, a spectacle of wondrous beauty, overwhelming to those who beheld it and unbelievable to those who only heard of it. The dome seemed not to rest upon solid masonry but to be hung from Heaven. He goes on to compare the stonework with a meadow full of flowers in bloom. The simile is not extravagant, for the richness and variety of the marbles with which the interior is faced are deliberate and magnificent. Another sixth-century writer, Paul the Silentiary, who hymned the re-dedication of 563, devoted 30 hexameters to the 12 diverse quarries which had contributed their yield. Eight gigantic pillars of green Molossian (*verde antico* from Atrax in Thessaly) lined the nave to north and south. Eight great monoliths in porphyry stood in the four exedrae (those in the south-east are best preserved) and came from near Egyptian Thebes. The tenth-century source already quoted (the Anonymous of Banduri) pretended that these were filched from ancient temples at Ephesus and Baalbek, but it seems unlikely that such evidences of Justinian's power would, if true, have been overlooked by contemporaries. Hagia Sophia has been standing for fourteen centuries, which is more than enough time for legends to arise, for guides and tourists to propagate them. In all there

Plate 24

Plate 25

are 104 columns, each a single piece of stone; 40 are in the nave and 64 in the galleries. The walls too are lined with slabs of carefully chosen and contrasted marbles. It is difficult today to conceive the refulgence which once existed: most of the west wall has recently been cleaned and gives some idea, but a better impression can perhaps be gained by a visit to the far smaller church of the Saviour in Chora, renovated since the war.

The original fittings of the church were of equal splendour. Procopius states that 40,000 lb. of silver were employed in the sanctuary (or *bema*) whose area corresponded with that of the apse, and was divided from the main body of the church by a screen, the iconostasis. The actual altar was of gold. The space in front was called the Solea. Under the east arch was a large ambo; this pulpit had to be reconstructed after the fall of 558, when it took the form of a circular platform, mounted on eight pillars, with steps to east and west, the whole richly decorated with silver and precious stones. In the south-east corner of the nave can still be seen in the floor a square set out in coloured stones and marbles: this work, of a rather Cosmatesque charac-ter, probably dates from as late as 1356 and indicates where the throne of the emperor was set for coronations. The normal seat of the sovereign was in the eastern section of the south aisle: his consort occupied the centre of the west gallery. Little is known about the mosaic decorations of the roofs and soffits of the arches in the church at this date, but the probability is that they were non-representational. A not altogether explicit sentence of Paul the Silentiary suggests that the dome was ornamented with a great cross. Wide use was made of rich hangings in the aisles and galleries. The gates were of bronze, often silvered over: two fine examples survive at the present south-west entrance. In short, nothing of lavish magnificence was spared for the 'Great Church', a name as often used as the dedication.

Under Justinian the cathedral was served by 525 clergy and the number soon rose to 600, including 80 priests, 150 deacons and lesser orders to match. Today the building is bare of priest, imam or any worship and it calls for an effort of imagination to fill it with the throng of clergy in their sumptuous vestments, matching the rich apparel of emperor and court, the aisles crowded with congregation and the gallery with women; thousands of flickering lights would find reflection in the polished walls, the silver fittings and the jewelry of priest and layman alike. A richer ritual can rarely have been offered than rose here with chant and incense to the Divine Wisdom of God in this His shrine.

The architecture of the interior has survived with little change other than the restorations outlined above. Fashions in decoration altered of course, and the effect of the iconoclast movement will be discussed later; so will the superb mosaics which followed the restoration of images. Disaster came to the church in 1204 when the Fourth Crusade broke into the capital. It was plundered mercilessly not only of gold and silver, but also of relics. None the less the feeble Latin Empire paid some attention to the outside of the building. They may have been responsible for some flying buttresses at the west end which projected into the courtyard (though German excavators assigned these to the ninth century), but they certainly strengthened the other three sides of the church with slender buttresses of a gothic type. In addition, urged by the predilection of the western church for bells, they erected a belfry in the middle of the west façade.

These fresh supports for the dome did not seem enough. Its pressure outwards was less since the increase in height by Isidore the younger (for the intensity of thrust by a dome varies inversely with the rise of its shell) but it was still considerable. In 1317 the Emperor Andronicus Palaeologus added four vast buttresses opposite the four main piers to take some of the weight. They are massive, more bulky than they need to be to do their work, and make it exceedingly difficult to appreciate the outside of the church.

In 1453 Mehmet the Conqueror converted the cathedral into a mosque. It kept its old name and became 'Camii Ayasofya ki, ber', the great mosque of Ayasofya. At first the belfry was prob, ably used as a minaret, then a wooden minaret was contrived over a turret on the west façade. In due course four independent minarets were set up. The earliest, at the south,east corner, is the only one in brick and was probably the work of the Conqueror. It is an unusual place for such a feature (the south of the main entrance is normal) and perhaps Mehmet II meant it to be a visible sign of triumph from the seaward side. Beyazıt II added another, of stone, at the north,east corner. Then towards the end of his life Selim II (1566–74) ordered the great Sinan to build one at the south,west corner; he died before the work was achieved and it seems likely that his successor Murat III decid, ed to make them into a matching pair at either end of the west front. It was also Murat III who brought into the church two great alabaster urns of Hellenistic workmanship which came from Pergamum and were set up in the western exedrae, for ablutions.

Within, the building had to be adapted to Islamic usage. The ambo was removed. A *mihrab,* the niche facing Mecca, had to be cut in the apse. The orientation of Hagia Sophia is something of a mystery. It does not face due east, but 33° south of east, a circumstance for which no wholly satisfactory reason has been produced. The direction of Mecca is however sub, stantially further to the south, as can be seen from the still exist, ing *mihrab.* Also erected was a *minbar,* a form of pulpit from which the imam could read passages of the Koran, gripping in the other hand a sword as was correct for a captured city; this was put against the south column of the apse. The floor was covered with carpets. In 1650 a famous Turkish calligrapher wrote an inscription in praise of Allah in the centre of the dome. What lies beneath is uncertain. One fifteenth,century traveller (Clavijo) speaks of a great figure of Christ Pantokrator, but no trace of this has been observed in recent years; it is unlikely that the Islamic record will lightly be removed. Gradually, all mosaics showing a human figure were covered with plaster. The south front of the great edifice allowed room for a series of Turkish tombs: within these *türbes* lie five sultans, three sultanas and 140 of their children – 102 stemming from the fertile loins of Murat III – many of whom were executed when their brother achieved the throne.

In 1847 Sultan Abdul Mecid became alarmed about the state of the imperial mosque. Two Swiss-born brothers, the Fossati, were invited to undertake survey and repair. They toiled for two years and made an invaluable series of drawings of what they saw. During the aftermath of the first world war, the Sultanate and the Caliphate fell in succession. Turkey was reorientated under the government of Mustafa Kemal. In 1934 Kemal announced that the building would become a museum, which was formally opened on 1 February, 1935. All practice of religion ceased, and this fabulous, enduring shrine welcomes today not the worshippers of Christ, nor the followers of Muhammad but the curious, the tourist and the regard of the informed.

Lethaby opens his seminal account of the cathedral by stating bluntly that 'Sancta Sophia is the most interesting building on the world's surface.' Even if the claim is overstated, some consideration of the place of Hagia Sophia in the story of architecture is necessary. It is above all a subtle building, which does not reveal its secrets to the brief or casual visitor. The artifice of Anthemius and Isidore conceals the grandeur and the size of the central space. If statistics aid, they reveal that the whole church of Sergius and Bacchus could be placed within that space and nowhere touch a wall or vault. Thomas Whittemore, who gave his life to the rehabilitation of the mosaics, loved to recall the English visitor, to that moment unmoved, who followed a leisurely pigeon with his stick and exclaimed, abashed, that it was out of shot. But we can ourselves pass along the broad galleries, or glimpse the towering dome between the porphyry columns. It is more difficult to discern whence this harmonious and unique concept sprang. The historians of art, seldom a unanimous band, have claimed a purely eastern origin for it, tracing domes back to Armenia and Mesopotamia and the territory of brick architecture, or have stressed the concrete vaults of Rome and the west while drawing parallels with the baths of Maxentius. As often, the truth is simpler: Hagia Sophia is a great stride forward in its own right, an incomparable and undisputed masterpiece, but it surges forward, not only in its materials but in its spirit, from the whole Empire. Precedents may be dragged hence and thence: the fusion is new and was the work of men of genius who were given their opportunity, as it was also given to Wren or to Sinan.

It may seem literally bathos to turn to one other aspect of the public works of the Emperor Justinian. We have seen how Valens elevated his aqueduct to bring water into the centre of the capital, and how great open reservoirs were excavated. To these Justinian added large underground cisterns. The best known of these was dug on a site near where a grand basilica had stood beside the Mēsē. The entrance today is just opposite the west front of Hagia Sophia; the voyager descends into a half-lit world of columnar vistas and the steady, stealthy drip of water, still clear and unsullied. In fact 336 pillars with a variety of capitals support brick vaults over an area about 140 m. by 70. The whole affair is obviously constructed with re-employed materials; since the pillars are 8 m. high, the cistern could have contained an enormous quantity of water against siege or drought, and is a romantic witness to the sophistication of Byzantine life at this period.

Plate 27

Only a quarter of a mile to the south-west, just off Divan Yolu, which follows the classic line of the Mēsē, is another

Fig. 16   Binbirdirek cistern. Possibly fourth century AD

Fig. 16

cistern. The Turks have a happy, poetic touch for describing Byzantine monuments; the Basilican cistern is Yerebatan Sara-yı – the palace under the water; the next is Binbirdirek – the 1,001 columns. It is smaller, and possibly older; tradition links it with the name of Philoxenus, a noble of the era of Constantine. Here in a space 64 m. by 57, stand 224 symmetrical columns, designed for the purpose, but the floor is dry and has indeed covered almost half the height of the pillars, thus allowing the curious to walk among them.

The great open tanks contained approximately a million cubic yards of water. The two dozen subterranean cisterns so far known – and there may be many more – were of varying sizes. Between them all, it was determined that the city of Constantine and of Justinian should not fall short of water, whether it was needed against fire or siege, for cultivation or for consumption.

Some authorities assign to the period after Justinian the Ka-lenderhane Camii, which has a simple basic plan of a single dome over a clearly cruciform interior. This building, perhaps to be identified with the monastery of Christ Akataleptos, was problably reconstructed in the ninth century and has within some fine fragments of marble decoration of this date. At the time of writing it is undergoing reconstruction.

CHAPTER IV

The Bastion of Europe

Perhaps the interpretation of the Koran would now be taught in the schools of Oxford, and her pulpits might demonstrate to a circumcised people the sanctity and truth of the revelation of Mohammed.   GIBBON, *Decline and Fall* Ch. LII

THE LONG REIGN and vast endeavours of Justinian left a legacy of financial and political disorder. This did not prevent further embellishment of the city in the sixth century. The general plan had been laid out by Constantine and Theo-dosius II: Justinian had added new glory to the focal point with his metropolitan church, which now dominated the north side of the Augusteum or central square. Here, Justinian had mounted a great equestrian statue of himself in imperial insig-nia on the summit of the column set up by Theodosius. By now there were five great columns in the piazza – one with a statue of the Augusta (St) Helena, in whose honour the place was named, one for Constantine himself, with his family group-ed round the base, the third erected by Theodosius and occu-pied by Justinian, a fourth for Eudoxia, the wife of Arcadius and a fifth for Leo I (457–74).

An English urban skyscape is punctuated by spires, the out-line of Istanbul today owes its character to the tall Turkish minarets; the stroller in Constantinople must have been very conscious of the profusion of pillars rising above street and forum, sometimes decorated with spiral scenes and in general crowned by the statue of their creator. In addition to the five columns there was also a great timepiece, the Horologion (one of seven distributed about the capital); it was ornamented with twenty-four doors of which one flew open each hour of the day and night – by what mechanism we are ignorant. Near by, as has been stated, was the Milion, from which all roads were measured: hence the stately line of the Mēsē, the main thorough-

Plate 26

65

fare, passed through the forums of Constantine, Theodosius, Bovis and Arcadius to the Golden Gate and the imperial road westwards. Just after the Theodosian forum, a bifurcation led north-west to the gate of Charisius and the route to Adrianople and the Danube lands. Other minor side roads linked with the gates in the massive wall. These streets would have been inhabited by the well-to-do and lined with the shops which served them. Almost nothing is known of the domestic architecture of the city. Beyond doubt the nobles lived in palaces of considerable splendour, ornate with marbles and mosaics; no doubt also the meaner classes lived in slum conditions, in alleys dark and steep, the seamy side of every cosmopolitan city in the world. Everywhere there were churches, mostly small. In about AD 430 only fourteen are listed: Justinian, according to Procopius, had a hand in building or restoring at least a score. All in all, the names of 485 are known, and many small shrines or mortuary chapels must have perished unrecorded. More than 100 were dedicated to the Virgin; of the angelic host St Michael was most popular, of earthly saints the Prodromos or Forerunner (St John Baptist) was followed by St Nicholas of Myra, the original of Santa Claus. At various dates there were 325 monasteries mentioned: but some of these were probably refoundations with a different dedication. Most had fallen into decay before the end of the Christian empire in 1453.

On the south side of the Augusteum was the entrance to the Great Palace which we must assume to have been the most sumptuous group of buildings in Constantinople. Access was through the Chalke, or Brazen House, which may have taken its name from tiles of bronze or from great bronze doors. It was a large domed structure and eventually (970) became a chapel. Destroyed in 532, it had been rebuilt by Justinian and adorned with an image of Christ. Within was a collection of statuary, gorgon heads from Ephesus, a gilt statue of Belisarius and effigies of various emperors. This portal must have stood in the south-east corner of the open space between Hagia Sophia and the mosque of Sultan Ahmet: north of it lay the Baths of Zeuxippus.

To western ears, the very term 'Great Palace' is possibly misleading. All idea of a massy block like Versailles or Buckingham Palace must be dismissed at once. The Byzantine palace was a loosely linked mesh of courtyards and pavilions, mostly of one story and covering a considerable acreage. Ultimately the area occupied by palace buildings was bounded by the length of the Hippodrome on the north-west and the sea on the south and east. The whole area now under the Blue Mosque and its dependencies, and a good deal of the open space north of it, was part of the palace complex. Within this area old buildings fell into disuse and new ones rose to replace them or satisfy the whim of an autocrat. From about the twelfth century the Great Palace ceased to be the main residence of the emperors, but it was never completely deserted. Thus it witnessed eleven hundred years of occupation with all the changes that such a time span can bring.

The whole subject is a tantalizing one. On the one hand the Great Palace must have been, in its heyday, a spectacle of extraordinary magnificence. Mysterious, in that its ground plan conformed to no scheme, and was furthermore on the side of a hill, confusing no doubt in the lack of system and level in getting from one place to another, the palace must also have had halls and vistas of extreme splendour and richness. On the other hand almost nothing remains of all this glory, and excavation is unlikely ever to reach firm conclusions because so many of the key sites lie under a huge mosque, itself a majestic work of art. Later writers, particularly the Emperor Constantine VII Porphyrogenitus, have given such full descriptions, that efforts can be made to reconstruct the sites of some of the main features, but nothing will fully recreate the courtyards and the fountains, the corridors and vaulted chambers, the numerous churches, nor re-people these pleasure-domes of dream with the moving pageant of the courts, the susurrating silks, the heat of the summer or the icy winters from the Black Sea. Allowing for alterations in style we must base our ideas on edifices such as the palace of Granada or the courts of Fatehpur Sikri.

The entrant through the Chalke left behind the open square of the Augusteum. To his right lay the Baths of Zeuxippus, which after serving as a species of museum had been allotted to the imperial silk factory. The establishment of this industry was another of the triumphs of Justinian. All silk had previously been imported from the East, but during his reign some eggs were smuggled into the Byzantine Empire (by two monks according to Procopius; but accounts vary) and soon the silkworm flourished on mulberry trees by the Bosporos; in later generations the rich and patterned textiles were a feature of the court and much-prized presents to the west. The factories at Constantinople were the most important and without doubt the most technically skilled. The Zeuxippus was, however, off the main path into the palace complex; this led through the headquarters of two units of the palace guards, the Scholae and the Excubitores. The Byzantine army was sharply divided between the provincial corps and those regiments stationed in the capital. These latter units were commanded by an officer called a Domestic; the Domestic of the Schools may not sound a very martial figure, but in Constantinople he was equivalent to the commander of, say, the Grenadier Guards in rank and duties. Near by was a church of the Apostles.

After this military region the oldest section of the palace lay ahead, the Daphne originally built by Constantine the Great. The position of this is fairly certain, for it adjoined the royal box in the centre of the east flank of the Hippodrome (the Kathisma) It was approached by a series of state apartments, some with resounding names, such as the Hall of Nineteen Couches, a banqueting room of basilican shape with an apse and nine

Fig. 17

recesses on each side containing couches on which the diners, in true Roman fashion, reclined. Near by were two Halls of Audience, the Greater and Smaller 'Consistoria', and other buildings acted as an archive repository and the treasury.

The palace of Daphne itself must have been approximately under the forecourt of the Blue Mosque. It certainly had one octagonal pavilion, and three churches or chapels (dedicated to St Stephen, the Trinity and the Virgin) were grouped round it. But the palace of Constantine did not suffice and lower down the hill other emperors added their own structures. Justin II (565–78) and his successor Tiberius were responsible for a splendid throne room called the Chrysotriklinos; it was octagonal with a cupola and may roughly have resembled San Vitale at Ravenna, or SS. Sergius and Bacchus in the capital; the interior was decorated with mosaics including one of Christ enthroned. The Chrysotriklinos continued to be an important centre of palace activity, and was added to by later emperors. Theophilus (829–42), who made a number of striking alterations to the palace buildings, put in a marvellous gold cupboard with five sides, in which a selection of the regalia was exhibited. Here too was the wondrous tree of gold and enamel, with singing birds, which lent inspiration to the Byzantine poems of W. B. Yeats:

> ...such a form as Grecian goldsmiths make
> Of hammered gold and gold enamelling
> To keep a drowsy Emperor awake
> Or set upon a golden bough to sing
> To lords and ladies of Byzantium
> Of what is past, or passing, or to come.

This last and lovely line is a fair definition of the continual process of reconstruction which went on among the ramifications of the palace area. Also somewhere on the slope below the Daphne, Theophilus built the three-apsed hall, on two levels, named the Triconchos and near it an open arcade called the Sigma. Not far from it was another reception hall, erected by Justinian II in 694 and known as the Justinianos. This hall we know to have been blown down in a storm in the fourteenth century: but we are ignorant of the precise fate of many of the surrounding buildings. Slightly to the north, Justinian II de-molished a church of the Virgin and built a courtyard and fountain (Phiale) designated for the use of the faction of the Blues. Near by he built a similar construction for the Greens. Those were however abolished by Basil I (867–86) who laid out a Bath, where the Blues had foregathered, and removed both fountains to the Nea church (*cf.* p.91).

The Nea was on a terrace, elevated on the hill which falls away from the Hippodrome to the sea. On the same level, but further south, stood three more churches, more or less side by side – St Demetrius, Our Lady of the Lighthouse and Saint Elias. The central one took its name from a beacon which stood a little above the 'House of Justinian', and served not only as a light to shipping entering the Bosporos from the Sea of Marmara, but also as a signal station which could flash messages across the water to Asia and be relayed to the further frontiers of Anatolia. In the ninth and tenth centuries it was claimed that, by a code of signals, news of a crisis in Cilicia could reach the palace within an hour.

Between the lighthouse and the Hippodrome is one of the few areas of the palace to have been scientifically excavated. Here, before and after the second world war, the Walker Trust of St Andrew's University was able to lay bare a large cloistered courtyard whose garths were decorated with floor mosaics. To the east of it was an apsed hall. Today these mosaics are preserv-ed in a special museum, and most of them are still *in situ*. They lie far below the level of the modern streets and reveal with start-ling clarity how complete have been the ruin and alteration of

Plates 28–30

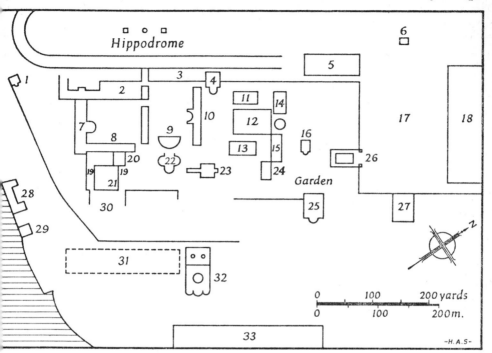

Fig. 17   Sketch plan of the Great Palace. This reconstruction is conjectural and omits many
buildings not mentioned in the text; it is based mainly on the edition by A. Vogt of the Book
of Ceremonies written by the Emperor Constantine VII

1 Church of St Peter
2 Covered Hippodrome
3 Kathisma
4 Church of St Stephen
5 Zeuxippus
6 Milion
7 Justinianos
8 Lausiakos
9 Sigma
10 Daphne Gallery
11 Triklinion of XIX Couches
12 Tribunal of XIX Couches
13 Greater Consistory

14 Guards' Quarters
15 Guards' Quarters
16 Church of the Apostles
17 Augusteum
18 Hagia Sophia
19 Imperial Apartments
20 Kainourgion
21 Chrysotriklinos
22 Triconchos
23 Karianos
24 Church of the Saviour
25 Magnaura
26 Chalke

27 Senate
28 Bucoleon Palace
   ('House of Justinian')
29 Pharos (Lighthouse)
30 Area of Walker Trust
   Excavations
31 Approximate site of
   Churches of St Demetrius,
   Our Lady of the Lighthouse
   and St Elias
32 Nea Church
33 Polo Ground
   (Tzykanisterion)

the palace area. The subjects are shown in isolation and without any consistent theme against a plain background. All are
secular, many are bloodthirsty: some portray buildings and
trees; several exhibit a marked sense of humour. A mule shedding its rider gives a pleasing example of this spirit. The technique of the mosaics is exceedingly accomplished and has no
parallel in the capital: if similar works are to be sought, they
must be found in North Africa. No shadows are used and
there is little feeling for perspective.

Unhappily it is not at all easy to date these works of art precisely. Their quality is beyond question, but it seems probable
that this court had already passed out of ordinary use when Constantine VII wrote his treatise. No clue as to the builder can
thus be won from the literary sources. At first archaeologists
ascribed them to an early phase, then they were assigned to the
period of Justinian. One modern critic has urged a date as late
as 700, but the most likely period and one confirmed on the
whole by the pottery fragments beneath them is the last part of
the sixth century AD.

Such artistic achievements, and the palace mosaics are by
any standards an impressive performance, remind us of two as-
pects of art. First, the capital was supremely the centre of the
Empire and the fount of inspiration. Here patronage flowed,
springing most bounteously from the occupant of the throne;
here conversely the most talented craftsmen assembled. Here
were practised to perfection the minor arts which still survive,
the purple codices, the jewelry, the ivories, the silverware, the
mosaics built up tessera by tessera, the foliated capitals; here
lesser craftsmen split the marble into panels, hewed the stone
and carried out the background work. Secondly, the strong
survival of classical spirit cannot be ignored. This it was that
first prompted an early dating for the palace mosaics and the
same feeling can be observed in the silver dishes, mainly hall-
marked to the reign of Heraclius (610–41) which still survive in

Plate 28

some numbers, mainly in the museums of Leningrad and Nicosia. Admittedly there is variation in quality, but the evidence is clear that Constantinople was the artistic hub of the Empire and dictated the style of the areas beyond. Faced with the evidence of the minor arts, we must regret all the more the harshness with which time and enemies have annihilated the secular architecture of the emperors.

The loss may be illustrated by a more detailed glance at one vanished building. Near the Chrysotriklinos of Justin II, already three centuries old, Basil I (867–86) put up the Kainourgion (literally the Novelty) which is described for us by his grandson the Emperor Constantine VII in his continuation of the earlier chronicle of Theophanes. This hall was of basilican shape, sustained by sixteen columns. Eight of these were of Thessalian marble, green in hue, six were of black onyx carved with vine tendrils and animals and the last pair, also of onyx, had spiral flutings. The campaigns of the Emperor were told in mosaic detail against a gold background. A square chamber next door, seemingly a bedroom, had a floor of variegated marble, so rich that it resembled a mosaic; in the centre was a peacock, set in Carian marble between four eagles. Basil I and his wife were depicted in the majesty of their imperial robes on one wall, their children – they had four sons, two of whom reigned while one became Patriarch – occupied others. All these figures raised their hands in adoration to the flat, gilt ceiling decorated with a great cross. It seems plausible that this gorgeous room was completed before the early death of Basil's eldest son in 879. If so, it emphasizes the long span of Byzantine history to recall that Constantine's palace of Daphne was already 500 years old and that the site of the Great Palace was to continue in Christian occupation for another five and a half centuries. The ultimate fate of the Kainourgion is not known.

The period after the death of Justinian saw the invasion of the Balkan peninsula by the Slavs and the renewal of wars against Persia. The imperial administration was short of money and struggling against popular resentment. Strife between the Blue and Green factions was again rampant. Discontent reached a head in 602 when the army on the Danube mutinied and proclaimed Phocas. The existing Emperor, Maurice, was dethroned and eventually murdered with his family: he was an able and generous man and had made a profitable peace with Persia, but this availed him nothing. His sons were slain before his eyes; with almost superhuman courage, Maurice revealed to the executioner that the nurse of his youngest was proferring her own babe to save the princeling.

The reign of Phocas, inexperienced, lecherous and treacherous, was a disaster. Persian armies broke through the eastern frontiers and their advanced units reached Chalcedon (609). Hordes of Avars and Slavs penetrated into Greece, despite efforts by Phocas to buy them off. Frequent conspiracies in the capital were put down with slaughter and reprisal. Pestilence and famine both added to the unrest, though they can scarcely be blamed on the incompetence of the ruler. Quarrels and plots were rife among the aristocracy; the lower orders were in a ferment of discontent and factious rivalry. Would the eastern half of the Roman Empire follow the western into dissolution?

HERACLIUS

Rescue came from an unexpected quarter. One of Maurice's far-sighted actions had been to reorganize the remnants of Justinian's conquests into two provinces ruled by Exarchs, at Ravenna and Carthage respectively. The Exarch of Carthage at this time was Heraclius and he boasted an heir of the same name. The son was equipped with a fleet by his father. During his voyage to Constantinople he was welcomed with acclamation and he had no difficulty in overthrowing Phocas. The new Emperor was young (36), fair-haired and vigorous, and his reign (610–41) marked a turning point in Byzantine history;

indeed to some historians of high repute it marks the beginning of Byzantine history proper.

The difficulties confronting the Emperor did not vanish overnight. The Persians continued their attacks, and though they were expelled from Asia Minor, they captured Antioch in 613 and Jerusalem a year later and with it the large portion of the True Cross which Helen had deposited there. In 615 the armies of Chosroes II were again at Chalcedon, and in 617 Persia invaded Egypt, captured Alexandria and deprived Constantinople of an important source of grain. At this juncture the Emperor was seized with despair. The imperial city seemed almost lost, the Sassanian hosts invincible; to the west the threat of the barbarian Avars was no less menacing. He decided to abandon Constantinople and transfer his capital to Carthage. From that wealthy and flourishing town he might be able to reorganize the defence of the Roman Empire. Secretly he loaded a fleet with treasures from the palace, and prepared his departure. The imperial destiny of Byzantium wavered, but fate was on her side. The fleet was wrecked by storms, and the news began to leak out. All over the capital it was received with amazement and protestation. The Emperor was compelled to change his plans; and the Patriarch bound him by a great oath, administered in Hagia Sophia, not to desert the Great City. J. B. Bury saw in this moment the turning point of the reign, and even conjectured a change for the better in the morale of the capital. Certainly the record of its inhabitants over the last two generations had not been inspiring. Bread and games were expected by the people, and the aristocracy had been grasping for power. The Patriarch Sergius, a powerful personality, allied himself with Heraclius and preached the struggle with Persia as a holy war. The Patriarch and the Byzantine Church were prepared to assist with their endowments as well as their prayers. In this great struggle against a heathen foe may be seen the first, dim foreshadowing of the crusading spirit.

The achievements of Heraclius were threefold. In the first place he must almost certainly be credited with a complete re- organization of the Byzantine provinces in Asia. Using no doubt his experience of his father's independent command in North Africa, he divided Asia Minor into districts known as *themes* in charge of which was a *strategos* – the classical Greek word for General – supreme in affairs civil and military. Se- condly, he effected a similar rearrangement of the civil service in the capital. This administrative revolution – for it was not much less – provided the personnel for running the Byzantine Empire in its greatest phase. Most important of all, these re- forms worked, and nowhere was the evidence clearer than in the Persian war.

The early disasters of the reign have been chronicled: Syria and Egypt had passed into the domination of the Sassanid king. The third great enterprise of Heraclius was his series of campaigns in the east. They were undertaken in person and between 622 and 628 he doggedly and systematically fought his way into the heart of the Persian kingdom. In 628 he was able to return to his capital in triumph, having sent ahead the Holy Cross which he later returned with pomp to Jerusalem. The lost provinces were regained, the holiest relic restored.

Nor was this all. The year 626 saw a formidable threat to Constantinople itself. Chosroes entered into negotiations with the Avars and once more despatched one of his generals with an army to Chalcedon. Heraclius, who was operating in Armenia, made no effort to check this invasion, other than detaching one third of his forces to the defence of the capital. The Persian corps arrived on the east of the Bosporos in June, and simul- taneously a great host of Avars, Bulgars and Slavs approached the land walls from the west; they were estimated at 80,000, and had brought shipping with them. The defence was in the hands of Bonus, a layman with the rank of Patrician, and the Patriarch Sergius, the strongest supporter of Heraclius. At the end of July the Chagan of the barbarians (who had already tried to kidnap the Emperor in 619) made an all-out assault. But the great walls were not breached and the enemy were driven back. On 3 August a fleet of rafts, designed to ferry across Persian troops to the European shore, was destroyed, and a week later a final assault by land and sea was defeated by Bonus and Sergius. Much credit was assigned to an icon of the Virgin, and the rude slumbers of the Chagan were said to have been haunted by visions of a richly clad female figure walking the inviolate battlements. Thus was dispelled the first serious threat to the walls of Constantinople; it was not to be the last. None the less, on his return Heraclius strengthened the land walls in the Blachernae area down to the Golden Horn where the land and sea walls met. This stretch was again reinforced by Leo V in 813. For it was the church of the Theotokos at Blachernae which housed the celebrated icon. Here too the Patriarch Sergius received the Holy Cross sent back by the Emperor.

If it was in 622 that Heraclius launched his campaign against Persia, the year is more memorable for a journey in Arabia. The prophet Muhammad made his celebrated withdrawal from Mecca to the city of Yathrib, later renamed Medina. It is the year from which the Islamic calendar still runs. Ten years later he died. According to a pleasing tradition, probably not well grounded in fact, the Prophet sent out letters in 628 to the Emperor at Constantinople and to the kings of Persia and Abyssinia, exhorting them to submit to the will of God – the meaning of 'Islam'. Chosroes II is reported to have sent an infuriated reply and Heraclius to have temporized with gifts. In any case the ruler of Byzantium was about to annihilate the Persian monarch. However, the generations of immediate successors to the Prophet witnessed an outward expansion of his faith which could scarcely have been foreseen by any contemporary.

THE RISE
OF ISLAM

Within ten years of the death of Muhammad, Damascus and Jerusalem were in the hands of his followers, and the True Cross was again in pagan hands, the Persian kingdom had been soundly defeated and Egypt and Alexandria occupied. Furthermore this startling, sensational expansion of the new Arabic faith launched a forked movement which threatened the Byzantine Empire in two directions. Northwards the thrust had seized Syria and all the holy places and also demolished the Sassanian kingdom; westwards the line of advance had captured the corn lands of Egypt and was extending towards the homelands of Heraclius himself – though Carthage did not actually fall into Muslim hands until 695. Sixteen years after the fall of Carthage the Arabs crossed into Spain.

It seemed as though the Mediterranean Sea might be encircled by a gigantic pincer movement. The city of Constantinople played the decisive part in preventing such an occurrence. In these developments the year 661 and the accession of the fifth Caliph, Muawiya, is of importance; he was the first Muslim ruler to cultivate sea power and build a fleet. The Arabs had been able to make frequent raids into Asia Minor, savagely disrupting the recently restored peace of the province there. In 670 they appeared in the Sea of Marmara, and seized the ancient town of Cyzicus on the south of the Propontis. For five consecutive years (674–78) the Islamic fleet sailed each summer up to the walls of Constantinople and attacked the city. Each time they were repulsed, and on the last occasion sailed away after incurring heavy losses. Again the walls had proved their strength, but the defenders were aided by a new and terrible weapon. It is in these naval campaigns that we first hear of the celebrated 'Greek Fire', invented by a Syrian refugee, one Callinicus. This violently ardent mixture, whose base was probably naphtha but which also included saltpetre, could be propelled from special instruments called siphons and would ignite when it struck its target. It would even burn on water. The nature of the compound and the manner of its propulsion were a jealous/ly guarded secret of the Byzantine state. Muawiya, now grow/ing old, was compelled to sue for peace and pay an annual trib/ute of 3,000 gold pieces. Even the Chagan of the Avars sent gifts and grateful messages of congratulation to Constantine IV And indeed his triumph was important; for this was the first occasion on which the apparently relentless tide of Muslim ex/pansion had been checked and turned back. Here, as two generations later, Constantinople was the saviour of European civilization.

Unfortunately, the success against the enemies from the east was followed by a failure in the north. During the seventh century a new branch of the Bulgar people crossed the Danube and settled in the area which still bears their name. An attempt by Constantine IV to expel them was unsuccessful: in later years the first Bulgarian Empire was a serious menace.

In Constantinople itself, the main preoccupation was once again with theology. The reign of Heraclius had seen the rise of the dogma of monotheletism, the concept that while the person of Christ had two substances, He had only one will (*thelēma*). It was hoped that this compromise might reconcile the many Christians of a monophysite flavour who lived in Syria and Egypt. Like many compromises, monotheletism did not achieve its ends; the expansion of Islam totally altered the political situation and also allowed a wide measure of toler/ance to the conquered Christian schismatics. Constans II, grandson of Heraclius, issued an edict in 648 (the Typos) which aimed at preventing further dispute. The Pope at Rome, Martin I, objected violently. Constans ordered his arrest; Mar/tin was brought to Constantinople, imprisoned and later exiled to the Crimea where he died. It was the last time that a Byzan/tine emperor was able so summarily to handle a Bishop of Rome.

In the autumn of 680 Constantine IV summoned the sixth
General Council of the Christian Church. It sat for almost a
year in his capital. Monotheletism was condemned and its
supporters excommunicated; they included one dead pope and
also the Patriarch Sergius to whom the city owed so much
fifty-four years earlier.

Constantine IV was succeeded by his son Justinian II (685–
95 and 705–11), the last of the Heraclian dynasty. We write of
dynasties in Byzantine history, but it must be clearly under-
stood that the succession to the imperial throne was by co-
option rather than by heredity. Justinian II, admittedly the only
son of Constantine IV, had been formally co-opted by his
father at the end of his life, and succeeded him because of this
fact and not by birthright. The new ruler was both devout and
tyrannical. He also spent much money on building, particularly in the Great Palace – some of his work there has already been
mentioned.

In 695 there was a revolt in Constantinople against the basileus (a style introduced by his dynasty): Justinian was exiled to
the Crimea, and his nose was cut off. His successor, a creature
of the Blues, was transient and embarrassed; as soon as an Arab
attack threatened, the Greens expelled him and brought in an
emperor of their own. These frequent changes of ruler indicated
the onset of a period of sorry instability. Justinian II had not
lost hope, and after a remarkable series of adventures he acquired first a Khazar wife and then the support of the Bulgarian
Khan. In 705 he appeared with his new allies outside the walls,
but could make no impression on them. Undaunted, the nose-
less emperor (Rhinotmetos, he was nicknamed) crawled into
his capital along an aqueduct pipe and put to flight his rival.
His second reign was ruthless, and the needs of the frontiers
were sacrificed to personal revenge. Only with Old Rome did
he make peace; a compromise was reached between him and
Pope Constantine, the last pontiff to be summoned to New

Rome, though its details are not recorded. In 711 another rising broke out and Justinian II found himself friendless. It was a sombre ending to a distinguished family.

Between 711 and 717 four emperors gained and three lost the imperial throne. Fortunately the last, Leo III (717-41) was capable of meeting the new crisis which was confronting Constantinople. Six months after the accession of Leo a great Arab army and fleet invested the city. The siege lasted for a year and was bitterly fought out. Maslama, the Muslim general, had advanced through Asia Minor at the head of 80,000 men and crossed into Europe over the Hellespont. Meanwhile a fleet of 1,800 vessels had sailed into the Sea of Marmara. Leo organized his defence brilliantly. We hear for the first time of a chain across the mouth of the Golden Horn to keep out hostile shipping. Greek fire was successfully used against the fleet of the enemy, and the land walls resisted all attacks. The winter of 717/8 was harsh, but no doubt oppressed the Arabs more than the inhabitants, who were accustomed to the inclement winds which blow down from the Black Sea in winter. The besiegers were reinforced in the spring, but kinder weather brought outbreaks of disease, and in August the forces of Islam withdrew. Once again the city had been saved.

The year 718 is a date of European, indeed world importance. The words of Gibbon at the head of this chapter apply to the victory at Poitiers a few years later of Charles Martel. The great siege of Constantinople in 717/8, following on the earlier triumph of 678 marked an infinitely more decisive check on the expansion of Islam. Arab sources aver that of 180,000 men engaged in the siege only 30,000 returned. Such figures must be regarded as a general indication of the scale of loss, rather than an accurate muster-roll. Constantine IV had delivered a potent check to the onrush of Islam; now Leo III had thrust it back. The consequences of defeat at this juncture are beyond calculation. As H. A. L. Fisher wrote:

If the Turkish conquest of Constantinople in the fifteenth century spread the Moslem creed far and wide through the Balkan peninsula, we may imagine the success which would have attended a Saracen conquest 700 years earlier, at a time when the peoples of Russia and the Balkans had received but a faint initial tincture of Christianity, and were still in a rude disorder of institutions and beliefs.

In truth the peoples of western Europe were in little better case. The opportunity for medieval society to emerge was guaranteed by the stout walls and brave hearts of Leo III and the garrison of the Great City.

CHAPTER V

Image Breakers and Image Makers

Carry me towards that great Byzantium
Where all is ancient, singing at the oars,
That I may look in the great church's dome
On gold-embedded saints and emperors...
Transfigured saints that move amid the fire
As in the gold mosaic of a wall.   W. B. YEATS, 'Sailing to Byzantium'

LEO III HAD SAVED Constantinople and the Empire. The story of his long campaigns in Asia Minor, which regained the *themes* there from the Arabs, does not directly concern the city. But a capital is of no value without rural backing sufficient to maintain it (Vienna is a recent case in point) and it must be stressed that the plateau, then fertile enough, which fills most of Asiatic Turkey today, was the best recruiting ground for soldiers and the most steady source of revenue to the Byzantine state. Its final loss in 1071 was a disastrous blow.

The main preoccupations of the capital were again theo- ICONOCLASM
logical. Leo III favoured a growing movement which frowned on the display and veneration of images, the Iconoclasts as they were styled. The idea came from the east and was of course paralleled in the stern Islamic prohibitions against the portrayal of the human form. The cult of icons had been increasing in the seventh century; the part played by the famous icon of the Virgin in 626 has been cited. More was involved than the mere display of sacred pictures in churches, monasteries and homes, for the icon was believed to be mystically associated with the saint depicted. Praise and prayer were offered to the icon as the proxy or symbol of Christ, the Virgin or the heavenly hierarchy. Some icons became credited with miraculous or thaumaturgic powers; beliefs of this kind were, naturally enough, uncritically accepted among the mass of the population, many of whom were fervent image worshippers – iconodules.

In 726 Leo III began to speak and preach against icons and in 730 he issued a decree proscribing them. Either in 730, or possibly earlier, he caused to be destroyed an image of Christ on the Chalke, an act which aroused widespread opposition. Even within the Church opinion was hotly divided. The monks of Stoudios were strongly iconodule; so was John of Damascus (St John Damascene); so was the Pope. John, living and writing peaceably in Muslim Syria, developed the theme of the icon as a symbol and mediator; some of his ideas were drawn from Neo-platonism, but they strongly influenced later thinking on this topic. In the capital, at least, a very considerable destruction of images must have followed. The University was closed in 726. Since in the long run the iconodules prevailed, the reputation of those emperors who were on the other side has suffered at the hands of the Church. All the popularity and honour which Leo had won in 717/8 evaporated before his ardent iconoclasm.

Leo's son Constantine V (741–75) was an even more fervent persecutor of images. At the beginning of his reign an iconodule rival got possession of Constantinople and was crowned by the Patriarch. But Constantine, like his father a brilliant soldier, outmanoeuvred and defeated Artabasdus. The pretender and his sons were blinded, but the turncoat Patriarch was only led round the Hippodrome on a donkey. Once again iconoclasm was supreme. To mark its triumph, Constantine summoned a Council, which met in a palace on the Asiatic shore of the Bosporos. He himself had written thirteen treatises against images; and they were utterly condemned by the Council, which was far from representative of the whole body of Christendom. '... there shall be rejected, removed and cursed out of the Christian Church every likeness which is made out of any material whatever by the evil art of painters.' A fresh orgy of destruction followed, and offenders were placed under the sanctions of the ordinary civil law. The famous church of the Theotokos at Blachernae, according to one source, became a fruit store and aviary. The feelings of the populace moved towards iconoclasm, for in 765 the abbot Stephen, leader of the image-worshippers, was torn to pieces in the streets of the great city.

The damage to works of art, and even to manuscripts, is beyond reckoning. Many monks migrated to Italy and so no doubt did painters and workers in mosaic. In the provinces, particularly those of the west, reactions were less violent. It is not an accident that at this period the Byzantines lost control of Ravenna (751) with the indirect consequence that the papacy had to look elsewhere for temporal protection.

For all Constantine's victories in Asia Minor and against the Bulgars, the capital was not immune from the assaults of nature. In 732 an earthquake caused considerable damage to the church of Eirene, and in 740 a more general tremor brought down a number of high statues, including that of Arcadius on his column and that of Theodosius I on the Golden Gate. The years 745–7 witnessed a terrible outbreak of plague, which seems to have arrived by sea from the east and to have been bubonic in character. The very interment of the dead became difficult and corpses had to be borne out of the city piled on rude platforms laid on pack animals. In 763/4 there was a particularly bitter winter, and pack ice drifted down from the Black Sea in such quantity that a jam was caused in the Golden Horn and across the mouth of the Bosporos; one giant iceberg was thrown against the sea-walls, which it seriously damaged. Two years later a severe drought reminded Constantine that the great aqueduct of Valens had been damaged in the Avar siege of 626, and he restored it thoroughly, collecting skilled workmen from various provinces of the Empire. But in general neither he nor his father were great builders.

Leo IV, the son of Constantine, was more moderate in his views; furthermore he married an Athenian, the Empress Irene,

who came from an iconodule province. Unhappily his prema-
ture death in 780 ushered in a distasteful twenty years of Byzantine history. Irene acted as regent for her son, Constantine VI, a
weak and pathetic figure. Gradually the formidable Empress
brought about a return of the icons. In 787 she assembled 350
bishops at Nicaea for the Seventh General Council, the last to
be recognized by both the Eastern and the Western churches.
Its proceedings were tolerant; iconoclast bishops who repent-
ed were welcomed back; it was carefully defined that veneration
was not to the icon but to the person depicted.

In 790 the army drove Irene out of the palace, but her son
foolishly allowed her back two years later. His own cruelty –
he removed the eyes of one uncle and the tongues of four others
– and military incompetence soon lost him his popularity. One
of the darkest deeds of Byzantine history followed. On 15 August, 797, the wayward boy was blinded by order of his own
mother in the same porphyry chamber where she bore him. For
five years, against all precedent, Irene ruled alone. It was during
this murky and ill-omened period that the Pope crowned
Charlemagne in Rome on Christmas Day 800. Much has been
written about this still enigmatic event, but at least Charles the
Great was sufficiently a realist to know that his title was worth-
less without recognition at Constantinople. This he did not ob-
tain until 811.

In the meantime a new threat assailed the capital. Ironically
enough, the successful campaigns of Charlemagne against the
Avars greatly increased the power and territory of their neigh-
bours, the Bulgars. The Emperor Nicephorus I marched against
them in 811, but he was disastrously defeated and his army destroyed. His skull was fashioned into a goblet for the triumphant potations of Khan Krum. Two years later Krum appeared before the walls of Constantinople, but was completely without resources to conduct a siege. This menace, alarming enough,
was less serious than the great attack a century before.

The successive emperors of the early ninth century are note-worthy for returning to iconoclasm, though with somewhat less enthusiasm and savagery than the first exponents of the move-ment. In 815 a synod held in Hagia Sophia reverted to the dog-mas of 754. Michael II (820–9) was an almost illiterate soldier, but his son Theophilus (829–42) was a character of more inter-est, and added to the beauties of his capital. He was interested in justice, and by tradition would roam the streets of Constantin-ople by night enquiring into the complaints of the citizens.

The sea walls, especially between the mouth of the Golden Horn and the Bucoleon palace, seem to have fallen into disre-pair. Almost every tower bears an inscription lauding the work of Theophilus in restoration. More exciting were his efforts in the palace. Rather to the north of the complex was a hall called the Magnaura, which was reputedly erected by Constantine in the first instance; it had become a place of meeting – the solemn, closing session of the Seventh Council took place here – and for the reception of ambassadors. Descriptions suggest that it was a large apsed hall with two aisles but its very position is uncertain, though it stood on a defined terrace. Here Theo-philus installed the wonderful devices which so impressed bar-barian and western envoys and which are famous from the de-scription of the Lombard bishop Luitprand of Cremona, who saw them in 949. Here stood the trees of gilded bronze in whose branches perched birds, each singing its own song. Further on, up six steps, was the emperor's state throne guarded by golden lions which beat the ground with their tails and uttered a terri-fying roar from their open mouths and quivering tongues. Seat-ed, silent and impassive on his great throne, the emperor was unmoved by these marvels. Dutifully the envoy would prostrate himself three times, only to find to his astonishment that throne and emperor had risen to the ceiling and that the basileus had changed his raiment. We may assume that the sophisticated Byzantine courtiers regarded these delightful ornaments as toys

THEOPHILUS

Plate 31

to dazzle the uncouth emissaries from beyond the frontiers of the Empire.

This cultivated ruler also created several buildings in the main palace – the Triconchos and the Sigma – mentioned above. A more typical iconoclast construction was a pavilion called the Pearl with marble columns and flooring and walls decorated with animal paintings. There the Emperor lived from spring till autumn and then moved to another sumptuous resi, dence, the Karianos, which must be presumed to have been better heated. His love of justice and dignity spared none: on one occasion he ordered to be burned a merchant vessel belong, ing to his wife, maintaining that an empress could not properly engage in commerce. In other circumstances seven children at, test his connubial affection, the compulsory curtailing of his courtiers' hair his common sense. Nor was he deficient in the arts of war. Twice his victories over the Arabs entitled him to a triumph (830 and 837): from the Golden Gate Theophilus rode in glory, preceded by his prisoners and followed by his adoring troops, along the Mēsē to the Augusteum. Here he dismounted from his white horse and entered Hagia Sophia to render thanks to God. Then he gave an address from the Brazen House, where not only a throne but an organ had been prepar, ed. All along the route the path was decked with flowers and rich carpets, and gold and silver cups were hung out to greet the Emperor. No doubt this was the common stuff of triumphs, but we happen to have been left unusually complete descrip, tions by a connoisseur of ritual – the Emperor Constantine VII in an appendix to his book on Ceremonies.

TRIUMPH OF THE ICONODULES Theophilus died in 842; in the following year his widow finally restored the images. In the western world the year 843 marks the treaty of Verdun and the first definition of the states which would develop into France and Germany; in the east it signals the ultimate triumph of orthodoxy. The actual day was Sunday, 11 March, and the Greek Church still celebrates the triumph of orthodoxy on the first Sunday in Lent of each year. Art and artists once more had a free hand, though it may be noticed that Byzantine religious art never welcomed statuary in the round. The greatest age of mosaic began; a new world of church building and church decoration opened out. We should not suppose that the iconoclast rulers did not decorate their ecclesiastical as well as their secular resorts. The evidence is lacking as far as Constantinople is concerned; but if mosaics as serene and lovely as those in the great mosque at Damascus (715), probably the work of Byzantine craftsmen, were set up in the capital during the iconoclast century, we can only deplore their loss.

Michael III, the Drunkard (842–67), is an enigmatic figure; his name has been blackened by the subsequent Macedonian dynasty as was that of Richard III by the Tudors. The truth seems to be that Michael was not a leader and could be led; at an early age he drifted into deep debauchery. Probably the great deeds of his reign were the work of others. His uncle Bardas refounded the University, allotting to it the Magnaura palace. The Patriarch Photius, perhaps the cleverest man to hold that post, boldly asserted his rights in face of papal claims; eventually he accused the Pope of heresy, for Rome had indeed introduced a phrase into the Nicene creed which had no historical place there.

For Constantinople, the crucial moment came in 860. A new enemy had appeared and from an unexpected quarter, the newly established Russian kingdom of Kiev; on 18 June their fleet, which had crossed the Black Sea, sailed out of the Bosporos and began an attack on the Great City. Russian contingents landed and surrounded the capital; the Emperor was away, but hastened to return; the Patriarch paraded the sacred robe of the Virgin; probably daunted by the walls, the Viking host melted away. Later chroniclers ascribed their defeat to a storm, but contemporaries say nothing of this phenomenon. More striking is the brilliant conception of Photius, that the right response to the Russian threat was to send missionaries to convert this new and alarming people. Michael III, to his own ultimate doom, had befriended a young groom called Basil; though styled 'the Macedonian' he was probably of mixed Slav and Armenian birth. Strong, illiterate, unscrupulous, this peasant horse-coper struck down in swift succession Bardas and his own benefactor. Attaining the throne by the foulest of deeds, he reigned glorious-ly, inaugurated a great epoch and founded the most celebrated dynasty of Byzantine history.

From 867 to 1056 the government of Byzantium was in the hands of the Macedonian dynasty; those rulers not descended from Basil I were related to his descendants by marriage; finally a popular affection for the family developed which may have prevented the replacement of its last, and unworthy, members by some more vigorous new stock. It was, unhappily, at that juncture that a combination of new difficulties confronted the state; but even unsuccessful emperors are sometimes triumphant in their patronage of art. Emerging from the shackles of Icono-clasm, and the discouragement of religious upheavals and reversals which characterized that period, Constantinople wit-nessed a fresh burst of activity and the splendid flowering of a new church architecture and the subtle vision of the mosaicist.

Two important additions were made to the score or so of churches in the palace grounds. In 864 Michael III totally renovated St Mary by the Lighthouse. This is described in a famous homily of Photius, which was formerly thought to refer to the Nea. The interior was profusely adorned with marble and mosaic. In the conch was a figure of the Virgin and in the dome that of Christ, possibly shown seated, rather than the later Pantokrator bust. Numerous other saints were portrayed. Here was a beginning of the highly stylized scheme of interior decoration which was to spread over the Empire in the eleventh century. No examples survive in the capital but Greece offers the series of Hosios Loukas, Chios and Daphni. At this shrine on Holy Thursday the emperor distributed apples and cinnamon to his dignitaries. Basil I (867–86) built a new church – the Nea – dedicated in 880; we know less of its details, but visitors such as the Arab traveller Harun-ibn-Yahya speak of its extreme magnificence. It lay rather to one side of the palace area, and was on a quincunx plan with five domes. Further north still, Basil erected a five-storied palace called the Mangana; it must have towered over the surrounding buildings, few of which were so tall. Beside it Constantine IX was later to put his church of St George. The Mangana was demolished at the end of the twelfth century; it lay east of the Saray kitchens but nearer sea level.

Basil I also restored a church of St Andrew near the cistern of Mocius; it seems likely that this was the edifice now known as Koca Mustafa Paşa Camii. Originally dedicated to the Apostle 'in Krisei', it also housed the relics of Hosios Andreas of Crete, a victim of the iconoclasts. Two capitals in the west aisle may go back to the sixth century, but the church was substantially restored in about 1284 by a niece of Michael VIII. When the Turks converted it into a mosque in 1486, they turned the axis of the building through ninety degrees and set the *mihrab* in what had been the south wall. The original plan, a central space with cupola surrounded on three sides by aisles, facilitated this arrangement; but the existing dome and two semi-domes are emphatically of early Turkish workmanship.

Leo VI (886–912) was called the Wise, since he was responsible for a great re-codification of the law. The main construction linked with his name was a church of Saint Demetrius, also near the Lighthouse. Seemingly it was square in form, and richly adorned with mosaics, while the floor of varied marbles suggested the waves of the sea. Here on the Saturday before

Palm Sunday, the day associated with Lazarus, the emperor distributed bouquets of palm leaves and spring flowers to his courtiers. Above all things, Leo desired a son to follow him. His first two wives died without giving him an heir. It was his misfortune that he had already promulgated a law forbidding third marriages. None the less he wed again, but fruitlessly. Then his mistress, Zoe of the black eyes, gave birth to a son. Despite the prohibitions of the Patriarch, Leo VI made her his fourth wife. He was forbidden to enter any church, and at Christmas 906 and Epiphany 907 the Emperor was turned back from the doors of Hagia Sophia. Obstinately he turned to the Pope, who held less stern views on multiple wedlock, and was ultimately able to have his son crowned and co-opted.

Constantine VII, the purple-born (*Porphyrogenitus*) (913–59) was not so styled without ironic reference to the circumstances of his birth. For much of his long reign power was in the hands of the former admiral Romanus I Lecapenus (920–44), his father-in-law and co-emperor. However, Constantine employed his leisure in writing a series of works which are absolutely invaluable to the Byzantine historian. Thanks to him we know in detail the attitude of the imperial administration to foreign states, and also the intricate life of ritual and ceremonial in which the emperor was involved. In one sense he was all-powerful; in another he was as much the prisoner of an unending series of official duties as he was physically confined in the rigid textiles of his priceless robes. On the 29th August he was bound to proceed by sea to the Stoudios monastery: on various days before Easter he distributed gifts, as we have seen above. Barbarian ambassadors had to be received in the Magnaura with the appropriate exhibition of mechanical toys. All round the city, other sanctuaries had their appointed days. Death made no difference. The defunct sovereign lay in state in the Hall of Nineteen Couches, where, living, he had so often banqueted. In due course the procession made its way to the Holy Apostles.

Here an official cried: 'Emperor, enter! The King of Kings and Lord of Lords summons thee.' Later he said, 'Remove the crown from thy head,' and the diadem was replaced by a plain purple fillet before the body was entombed in a sarcophagus.

The earliest emperors were interred in porphyry, but supplies of this rare stone from Egypt began to give out in the middle of the fourth century. A splendid group of early sarcophagi has been assembled outside the Archaeological Museum, but they are not assignable to particular autocrats. Within is shown what may plausibly be a fragment of the tomb of Constantine the Great. The identification is certainly more convincing than that which associates an elaborate Hellenistic shell from Sidon with the all-conquering Alexander.

Plate 32

For all the splendour of building, the imperial city was not immune from attack in the tenth century. In 904 a formidable Saracen fleet all but penetrated into the Marmara. In 913 Symeon of Bulgaria brought his array up to the walls but was daunted by them; in 924 he tried again but without success. That autumn Romanus I summoned him to an interview, held on a jetty in the Golden Horn. Symeon arrived on horseback, Romanus by water. Under the shadow of the pillars and domes of the Great City the Byzantine reminded the barbarian ruler of his obligations as a Christian, spoke of the Day of Doom and required Symeon to cease shedding Christian blood. Symeon was impressed and ceased his attacks; in fact he had exhausted his resources. In 907 and 941 Russian fleets appeared from the Black Sea; on the first occasion they were bought with a treaty of commercial privileges, on the second they were militarily routed, partly by the help of the terrible Greek Fire which caused appalling damage to their ships and sailors.

Within the security of the walls of Anthemius the building of churches continued. Time has dealt harshly with many of them, and even where remains are substantial, it is far from easy

Fig. 18

93

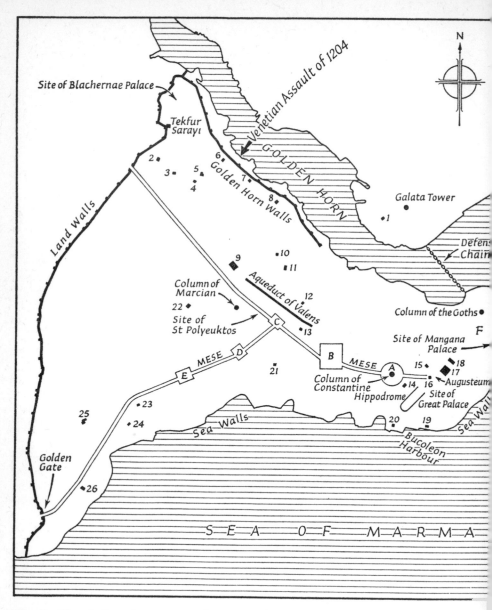

N

Site of Blachernae Palace

Tekfur
Sarayı

Venetian Assault of 1204

GOLDEN HORN

Galata Tower

Defens
Chair

2

3

5

4

6

1

8

Golden Horn Walls

Land Walls

1

10

11

9

Column of
Marcian

Aqueduct of Valens

12

Column of the Goths

F

22

Site of
St Polyeuktos

C

13

Site of Mangana
Palace

MESE

D

B

MESE

A

15

18

17

E

21

Column of
Constantine

14

16

Augusteum

Hippodrome

Site of
Great Palace

Sea Wall

25

23

24

Sea Walls

20

19

Bucoleon
Harbour

Golden
Gate

26

S E A   O F   M A R M A

Fig. 18   The main Byzantine monuments of Constantinople

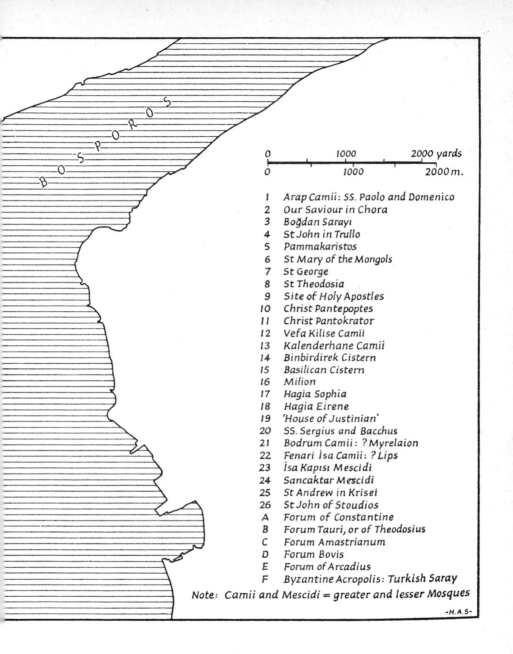

B O S P O R O S

| 0 | 1000 | 2000 yards |
| 0 | 1000 | 2000 m. |

1   Arap Camii: SS. Paolo and Domenico
2   Our Saviour in Chora
3   Boğdan Sarayı
4   St John in Trullo
5   Pammakaristos
6   St Mary of the Mongols
7   St George
8   St Theodosia
9   Site of Holy Apostles
10 Christ Pantepoptes
11 Christ Pantokrator
12 Vefa Kilise Camii
13 Kalenderhane Camii
14 Binbirdirek Cistern
15 Basilican Cistern
16 Milion
17 Hagia Sophia
18 Hagia Eirene
19 'House of Justinian'
20 SS. Sergius and Bacchus
21 Bodrum Camii: ? Myrelaion
22 Fenari İsa Camii: ? Lips
23 İsa Kapısı Mescidi
24 Sancaktar Mescidi
25 St Andrew in Krisei
26 St John of Stoudios
A   Forum of Constantine
B   Forum Tauri, or of Theodosius
C   Forum Amastrianum
D   Forum Bovis
E   Forum of Arcadius
F   Byzantine Acropolis: Turkish Saray

Note: Camii and Mescidi = greater and lesser Mosques

-H.A.S-to identify them certainly with the written accounts. To the west of the city, a little chapel, whose Turkish name was San-caktar Hayrettin Mescidi, survived in tolerably good order un-til the earthquake of 1894. Generations of antiquaries identified it with the convent of Gastria founded by the mother-in-law of Theophilus, but the evidence for this is scarcely convincing.

Plate 33

Something of the same problem surrounds the far more in-teresting church known today as Bodrum Camii. It has often been regarded as the Myrelaion monastery, founded by Roma-nus I as a burial place for himself and his family, but this rests on slender grounds. The design is unusual since two churches stand one above another, a rare feature in Byzantine art; the lower seems to belong to the seventh century, but the upper one is a narrow, elegant affair of what is called the cross-in-square pattern. The central dome stands over the intersection of choir, nave and transepts, but the four corners are filled in to give an almost square ground plan. It was an arrangement which found increasing favour. The building became a mosque to-wards 1500, but was badly damaged by fire in 1911. Today its bare skeleton gives an unusually clear impression of the archi-tecture, and interesting excavations have taken place around it. To the north lies an extensive and fascinating cistern, now dry, which seems to have served also as the foundations for an early circular structure of uncertain purpose. Quite recently a most romantic discovery was made. Among the debris from digging, Dr Nezih Fıratlı, of the Archaeological Museum, identified a fragment of porphyry as being the missing foot from the well-known sculpture of the four tetrarchs on the south façade of St Mark's at Venice. A Constantinopolitan origin for this splen-did group has long seemed likely; the main part was no doubt 'acquired' by the Venetians in 1204; but it does not necessarily follow that the whole once adorned the church on this site.

Plate 34

The dating and ascription of Byzantine churches is made no easier by the long period for which they often remained in use and the alterations which took place from generation to generation. The complicated edifice, now called Fenarî Isa Camii, is a case in point. Today it comprises two churches, side by side, with an L-shaped structure providing an outer narthex to both and a discrete south chapel. There can be no question that the northern church is another cross-in-square tenth-century benefaction, possibly due to the piety of Constantine Lips (d. 917). The southern church seems to have been added by the Empress Theodora (d. 1304), widow of Michael VIII, and dedicated to the Prodromos (St John Baptist). Many members of her family were buried there, and 32 burials were found in the 1929 excavations. Theodora's church is of a different pattern; the space under the central dome is surrounded by two aisles joined by an ambulatory. The outer narthex and south chapel are probably a generation later. The brickwork at the east end is redolent of the Palaeologue period. After becoming a mosque before the end of the fifteenth century, the complex was damaged by fire in 1633, and again more seriously in 1918. It is difficult to get inside today. A beautiful inlaid stone icon of St Eudoxia (probably twelfth century) was found here and is now in the Museum.

Plate 35

Equally difficult to date exactly is the large building overlooking the Golden Horn and known today as Gül Camii (Rose Mosque). It is customarily identified with the church of St Theodosia, an iconodule martyr on whose feast the Turks finally broke into Constantinople. Traditionally, they found her church packed with worshippers and decorated with roses. The main body of the church belongs perhaps to the late ninth century, but the central dome was rebuilt in Turkish times, and the most attractive feature today is the brickwork at the eastern end which must belong to a fourteenth-century reconstruction.

Plate 36

All three churches lack their interior decoration. Fortunately, as soon as the Iconoclast crisis was over, the ornamentation of Hagia Sophia began again. It is clear that the iconodule

HAGIA
SOPHIA
MOSAICS

party had to move slowly in the mob-ridden capital; and there may have been a scarcity of competent technicians. Accordingly, the earliest mosaics in the Great Church, dating probably from about 850, are concealed in a little-used chamber over the south-west porch. They include a Deesis – a common Byzantine theme showing Christ between the Virgin and the Prodromos, – Apostles, and portraits of patriarchs such as Tarasius and Germanus who had suffered for their support of images. A little later, probably in 867, came the fine figure of the Virgin in the apse; this presents some difficulty as it does not altogether match the description given in a sermon of the Patriarch Photius, but the weight of opinion supports this date. Around 900 may be placed another dramatic composition over the main entry door from the narthex. Here is shown an emperor, usually accepted as Leo VI, prostrate before Christ seated on a throne, between medallions of the Virgin and the Archangel Gabriel. The humility of the Emperor emphasizes none the less his position as an intermediary for his people. A minor technical point has recently been noticed in the work of this mosaic: two kinds of red tesserae were used, one more expensive than the other; the cheaper variety, on the scarlet shoes of Leo for example, has faded sadly.

More precise in chronology is the recently uncovered mosaic of the Emperor Alexander (912-3) in the north gallery. It is scarcely conceivable that anybody would wish to honour this horsey and unsatisfactory despot, save during his brief reign.

Over the south entrance to the narthex, that used by contemporary visitors, is a mosaic tympanum of greater historic interest. In this bold epitome of its story the protectress and patroness of *see Figs. 4, 9* the Great City, the Holy Mother of God, is seated between two standing and imperial figures; Constantine presents a model of his city, Justinian offers his church. Whittemore put forward a date of about 990, when it is known that the cathedral was undergoing repairs; there seems every reason to accept this. The drawing can also be related to a large group of manuscripts executed in the reign of Basil II; it has been suggested that this striking group may commemorate his drastic victory over the Bulgars in 1017.

The remaining compositions are all in the south gallery and fall into three groups, of which two are easily datable and the third more difficult. At the end of the gallery nearest to the vanished altar are the figures of the Empress Zoe and her third husband Constantine IX Monomachus (1042–55) on either side of Christ enthroned. A manifest interference with the inscription suggests that the work was originally completed in the reign of Zoe's first husband Romanus III (1028–34). It would seem that his head was then replaced by that of Constantine; traces of alteration hint that the Empress, who prided herself upon her unwrinkled complexion, had a face-lift at the same time. The richness of the imperial apparel is illustrated in Constantine's robes, but though the figures themselves are flatly treated, the onlooker has a vivid impression of true portaiture in the faces. Constantine was a patron of the arts; in addition to founding the Nea Moni on the island of Chios, he built a church of St George by the Mangana palace which evoked sardonic descriptions from Psellus, the finest historian of the age. The Emperor kept on changing the design, but finally beauty was achieved which 'pervaded every part of the vast creation, so that one could only wish it were even greater'. Spacious lawns, ornamented with series of fountains, surrounded the monastery, where Constantine was in due course buried.

Plate 37

The neighbouring panel shows a later royal family. On either side of the Theotokos stand John II Comnenus (1118–43) and his Hungarian wife Irene, and the mosaic was probably set up at the beginning of his reign. Again we can recognize in his fine, but severe, countenance the ruler of proved ability, normally rated the ablest of an able dynasty. It can also be seen that ever smaller tesserae are being used in the faces. At an angle, and possibly a few years later, was added the portrait of their son Alexius, a frail prince who predeceased his father.

Plate 38

The third mosaic in the gallery is the most beautiful in Hagia Sophia. It represents the Deesis and though it has been badly mutilated, the upper parts of the three figures survive to give an astonishingly vivid and individual depiction of Christ, the Virgin and the Baptist. Sharp controversy rages over the date. Some scholars prefer the early twelfth century, which seems to me more likely; others argue the quite recognizable similarity with early fourteenth-century work in Our Saviour in Chora. Once we are in front of it the serene beauty of the composition distracts the attention from chronological argument. The humanity and humility of the Prodromos contrast with the majesty of the Christ and the tenderness of the sadly damaged Virgin. It is a sombre speculation that there may once have been vast wall surfaces covered with work of this quality.

Constantinople was the centre of a wider domain under Basil II (976–1025) than at any time since the advent of Islam. A series of warrior-emperors had campaigned in triumph to west and east. In 944 John Curcuas, the ablest general of the day, brought back in triumph from Edessa an impressive relic, the 'mandylion' or towel bearing a likeness of the face of Christ. It was received with solemn thankfulness at the church of the Virgin at Blachernae, but later moved first to Hagia Sophia and then to the Virgin by the Lighthouse. In 961 after a ferocious campaign Crete was recaptured, with beneficial results for the commerce of the capital. The general here was Nicephorus Phocas, who later became Emperor and married the glamorous Theophano, his predecessor's widow. It was a union of contrasts, for he was ascetic, and, for all his military talents, probably somewhat grubby; the Empress was of low birth, of doubtful morals, beautiful and ambitious.

After six years of rule Nicephorus became increasingly unpopular. A conspiracy was formed under another soldier John

Tzimisces, in which Theophano seems to have been involved; it is however doubtful whether the two were actually lovers, as some alleged. The night of 10/11 December, 969, was bitterly cold and the Emperor retired early. Several important palace officials were absent or had been lured away. Towards midnight a small boat approached the Bucoleon harbour and a furtive group were hauled up by an accomplice from within. Silently they crept through the passages of the sleeping palace to the bedroom of the autocrat. There was an instant of horror when the bed proved empty, but the hardy Nicephorus was slumbering on a leopard-skin in the corner. Brutally he was aroused and done to death. Next day the city awoke to a new ruler, the engineer of a faultless *coup d'état* and a bloody assassination.

cf. Plate 19

Typhoid carried off John I in 976 and the youthful Basil II was able at last to take up the government. He proved to be an even more talented commander in the field; but the early years of his reign were plagued with revolts by the military aristocrats of Asia Minor. In 987 the young Emperor faced an apparently overwhelming menace from across the Bosporos. By a daring stroke he called to his aid a contingent of Russians, and defeated the rebels. The hitherto pagan and inimical Russians were moving into a new role. Vladimir, their prince, though of barbarous and licentious habits, did not lack a sense of the future. According to tradition he hesitated between adopting Western Christianity, Judaism, Islam or the faith of Byzantium; the lustrous liturgy of the Great Church swayed him to the last-named. For the first time, a purple-born princess was given to an alien, and Basil's sister Anne became the reluctant bride of the lord of Kiev. The results of Russia's entry into the orthodox fold are part of the pattern of world history. Some of their scholars have maintained that, if Constantinople was the second Rome, then Moscow was the third. It is ineluctably true that the rulers of the 'third Rome' have long coveted possession of the second for both historical and geographical reasons.

In maturity Basil II was a constant campaigner, at first on the eastern front and later against the Bulgars, with such success that he won the epithet of Bulgar-slayer. Unfortunately, he was celibate and the remaining members of the Macedonian dynasty were unable to cope with a coincidence of formidable problems. These do not directly concern the fate of Constantinople, but they may be summarized as the arrival of new enemies on both flanks of the Empire – the Normans in southern Italy and the Selçuk Turks in the east—increasing difficulty in controlling the great territorial nobles of Asia Minor and in preserving the free peasantry who constituted the best soldiers and the steadiest tax-payers, worsening relations with the Western Church, and a growing dependence in marine affairs on the sea power of Venice. These complicated issues called for high statesmanship and vigorous leadership, which, alas, were lacking. The affection of the populace for the Macedonian dynasty brought to the throne two women, one vain and one incompetent; the husbands of Zoe were not equal to the situation and the celibacy of Theodora proved no more successful.

In 1054 a breach with Rome took place; to contemporaries the schism did not seem as final or as serious as it subsequently proved to be. In 1071 the Byzantine army, under Romanus IV suffered at Manzikert, near Lake Van, an utterly catastrophic defeat by the Turks. The rich and military provinces of Asia Minor were lost for ever. Once again it seemed as though the days of the Empire were numbered and the position of Constantinople imperilled. A swift succession of mediocre emperors, promoted either by the armies or by the civil aristocracy of the capital, brought no relief. But once again the situation produced a great man at the moment of crisis. Alexius Comnenus (1081–1118) saved the state, founded a distinguished dynasty and engendered a daughter whose biography has enshrined her father's fame.

CHAPTER VI

The Last Age of Byzantium

Indeed you should know that they gazed well at Constantinople, those who had never seen it; for they could not believe that there could be in all the world a city so rich, when they saw those tall ramparts and the mighty towers with which it was shut all around, and those rich palaces and those tall churches, of which there were so many that nobody could believe their eyes, had they not seen it, and the length and breadth of the city which was sovereign among all others.   VILLEHARDOUIN, *The Conquest of Constantinople,* § 128

BY MEDIEVAL STANDARDS Constantinople was a vast city. Contemporary Rome housed a negligible population huddled among antique ruins; London and Paris were overgrown villages with scant amenities. The size of the population is very difficult to estimate. It used to be thought that, in the heyday of the Macedonian dynasty, not far short of one million people lived within the walls. Later estimates have been smaller, but a figure of 600,000 in periods of prosperity seems not unreasonable. Naturally the total varied with plague or war. There was in 542 a disastrous outbreak of plague, which recurred four or five times in the sixth century, in which the casualties have been reckoned at 225,000. Plague struck again in 745, and the Black Death was to reduce an already diminished population in 1348–50. By any standards, the size of Constantinople was considerable; it is probably not a gross exaggeration to suggest that in AD 1000 about as many men and women lived within its walls or in the suburb across the Golden Horn as inhabited England.

This population was highly cosmopolitan. Greek might be the spoken language, but peoples from all the wide bounds of the Empire mingled in the Great City and many from beyond it. Slavs, Armenians, Syrians, Jews might be expected, but rubbing shoulders with them would be great blond Varangians of the emperor's guards (many English fled hither after Hastings),

Negroes, Venetians and other Italian traders, Bulgars from the northern frontier who wore a metal chain around the waist in lieu of a belt, barbarians from further north – Russians, Khazars or Pechenegs, – Muslim travellers in turbans (fairly rare as far as we know at this date), and from everywhere the merchants whom the city attracted by its international commerce. Among these would pass the Byzantine nobles in their gorgeous robes, whose pattern and colour could indicate their rank, and their ladies, sibilant with silk and glittering with gems.

Heavy customs duties were levied on all imports and exports, normally at the rate of 10 per cent. This tax provided a major source of revenue to the government, but from the end of the eleventh century exemptions granted to Venice and others weakened its force. From every quarter goods passed through the city; from the north came furs and honey and amber, from the east spices, porcelain and jewels, from the south gold, corn and porphyry. Even the west contributed some raw materials and perhaps salt fish, though to an increasing extent it was absorbing luxury goods. The city knew no restrictions on imports (except, rather curiously, soap in order to protect the home industry). Within the capital, trade was closely organized. Each industry was governed by a guild which controlled prices and guaranteed craftsmanship. In general the purveyors of a commodity were grouped in one area. Horse dealers met round the Amastrianum forum, pig and cattle dealers thronged the forum of Theodosius. Bakers were on the Mēsē between the forums of Theodosius and Constantine, silversmiths also on the Mēsē but nearer the Augusteum. Not surprisingly, the fish market was on the bank of the Golden Horn; then, as today, the citizens bargained and enjoyed the constant supply of admirable fresh fish.

The deep interest of the ordinary citizen in religion needs no comment in the light of the many riots of the Iconoclast controversy. As the centuries wore on, this crystallized into a passionate support for the orthodox doctrines of the Greek Church. In vain, during the declining years, might the emperors seek union with Rome for political reasons or hope of military support; the ordinary folk would have none of it. This preoccupation with worship was coupled with many forms of superstition. Until 1204 the city was endowed with an unequalled richness of relics of Christ and the Apostles. But veneration was also given to later saints, to icons, even to pillars and stones. One column in Hagia Sophia was reputed to cure complaints of the eye. The column of Theodosius was believed to foretell the fate of the city. Signs and omens were observed and could cause panic. In the bitterness and agony of 1204 the people destroyed the great bronze statue of Athene by Phidias which stood in the Augusteum and fell under suspicion because it faced west and seemed to beckon the crusaders. In the last days of the capital fog and eclipse foretold the doom to come.

Alexius I (1081–118) successfully accomplished a great task of reconstruction, which need not concern us here, though the military pressure of Norman and Turk still subsisted on the two flanks of the reduced Empire. The next serious threat to the capital came in fact from the north. The Patzinaks (or Pechenegs) were a people of Turkish stock dwelling north of the Black Sea, but moving south. In 1090 a host of them reached the wall of Constantinople, which was also attacked from the sea by the Turkish Emir of Smyrna. Through the winter of 1090/1 the situation was desperate; the siege was tight and the Emperor helpless, or almost. Alexius resorted to a typical stroke of Byzantine diplomacy: leaders of another barbarian race, the Cumans, were invited to the aid of the Empire and responded so well that the Patzinaks were all but annihilated in a single bloody battle in April, 1091. It is possible, though by no menas certain, that in this emergency Alexius also despatched a *cri de cœur* to Robert, Count of Flanders, in western Europe; and

THE
COMNENI

that this message was in a sense the genesis of the Crusades, which must be discussed later. If so, nothing reached Constantinople from that quarter until the arrival of Peter the Hermit in August 1096, and this ill-disciplined and beggarly horde was of no advantage to the Emperor. Only later in the year did the first military units begin to arrive, with the expressed aim of liberating the Holy Places, not of helping Byzantium.

Despite the political and economic difficulties of the Comnenian age, there was a great resurgence of church-building. Most of the churches which survive in some order today were either founded or lavishly restored in this epoch. An outstanding example of the phases of Byzantine art is the church of St

Plate 47

Saviour in Chora, better known as Kariye Camii, whose origins go back by tradition to the age of Justinian, if not earlier; at all events a complete reconstruction occurred in the time of Alexius and this was in turn replaced by another restoration at the start of the fourteenth century, which gives the church its present character.

The church of Christ Pantepoptes, the All-Seeing, known today as Eski Imaret Camii, was certainly founded in about 1087. It is a smallish affair, today a Turkish school, but with an interior which has not been greatly altered. The dome, oc-

Plate 39

tagonal on the outside, rests on four pillars; the transepts are slight; the eastern apse has two small side-chapels, while the west end covers the narthex with a gallery. There is a rather dark exonarthex. On the south side, the only façade easily visible in a rather built up area, is some very attractive brickwork including a bold key pattern. Pantepoptes stands well, which led Alexius V to make this neighbourhood his headquarters during the last defence of the city against the Fourth Crusade.

Another even smaller church of the same sort of date is St

Plate 40

John in Trullo (near Pammakaristos), today a rather pathetic affair housing some rather scraggy chickens. It belongs, on a miniature scale, to the same ground pattern as the Pantepoptes.

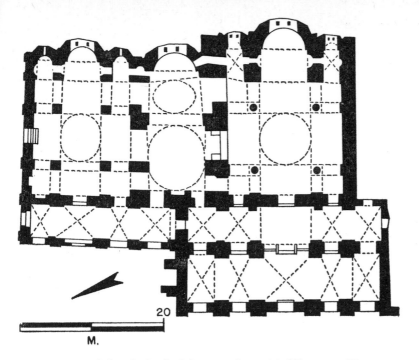

Fig. 19 Ground plan of Church of christ Pantokrator. Twelfth century AD

One must imagine medieval Byzantium dotted with chapels on this scale, less lengthy than a cricket pitch. More equivocal in date is the equally tiny church of Boǧdan Sarayı, which might be of twelfth-century origin, repaired two hundred years later. It has a doubtful element of romance since it has been vaguely identified with a chapel of SS. Nicholas and Augustine established by an Anglo-Saxon noble in the Varangian guard.

The church of Christ Pantokrator, the Ruler of All, (Zeyrek Kilise Camii) is a much more complex and grandiose foundation, closely linked with the Comnenian dynasty. The monastery was founded by the Empress Irene or her husband John II, whose mosaics appear in Hagia Sophia. Today it stands bravely on the scarp above the Atatürk Boulevard; the interior

Plate 41

107

Fig. 19

Plate 41

(closed at the time of writing) is in fact composed of three distinct churches side by side. That to the north was the work of John and Irene and must have been constructed during his reign (1118–43); it has a single dome on four pillars, making a centre-piece for nine compartments of which the eastern three have apses. The southern church is somewhat later, larger and more lavishly ornamented, but it presents a similar ground plan and can be dated to about 1180. The middle section is seemingly latest of all (though the other two must have presented a curious picture before, since their narthexes were contiguous) and was probably the mausoleum, dedicated to St Michael, of the dynasty, many of whom were buried here. The southern church has a very elaborate pavement in *opus sectile*. The whole arrangement is typically Byzantine in manner; where the western world would have rebuilt on a more splendid scale, or thrown out a lady chapel, the eastern architects of this period extended sideways. We shall meet this adding of a side-chapel (*parecclesion*) to a main church again.

The Comneni did not confine themselves to ecclesiastical benefactions. For some reason they wearied of the great palace to the south-east of the Hippodrome and began a new imperial residence in the northernmost angle between the walls and the Golden Horn. This was the Blachernae quarter where already stood the church housing the Sacred Veil of the Virgin. Some ceremonial chambers had been built here in the fifth century, but Alexius Comnenus was the first to establish a major palace. Here, for example, he was able to receive the leaders of the First Crusade. Only a former prison bastion, set against the wall and known as the Tower of Anemas (from an early occupant), remains of all this splendour. Fuller oblivion has overtaken the second, seemingly separate, palace put up near by for his grandson the Emperor Manuel (1143–80); by all accounts it was of great magnificence, and was probably nearer the Golden Horn. From now on emperors lived more and more in this quarter, and tended to desert their original home. This growth in the Blachernae quarter resulted in a need to expand outwards the existing city walls. Part of the extension, which makes a notice able bulge at the northern end of the land walls, can be ascribed to Manuel I, while part seems to be of Palaeologue work. It is no longer possible to determine the original line of the Theo dosian wall.

Three sovereigns of the Comnenian family held the throne for all but a century, and all were able. It was a remarkable record of statesmanship and military talent; and, as we have just seen, the capital was notably beautified under Alexius I, John II (the ablest of the three) and Manuel I (1143–80). The last nam ed leaned more to the west than any previous emperor, enjoyed tournaments, invited visitors to Constantinople and married two western wives. Unhappily, towards the end of his reign, he suffered a catastrophic defeat at the hands of the Turks (Myrio cephalon, 1176); his immediate successors, mainly men of les ser calibre, were not equal to the emergencies which arose. One strange and brilliant figure sought to arrest the tide of events. Andronicus I, witty, charming, sensual, a notorious amorist, greedy for power, altogether without scruple, had lived sixty adventurous years. The revolt in Constantinople which brought him to the throne also unleashed a hideous massacre of Latins living in the city. Many of the right remedies were applied vig orously by this extraordinary man, but with a ruthlessness which brought terror and uncertainty in its train. This malaise in the city was enhanced by the approach of a Norman army which had already sacked Salonika with professional brutality. In 1185 Andronicus was horribly murdered by the same mob which had welcomed him three years before.

The stage was now set for perhaps the greatest disaster in the history of Constantinople. Reference has been made (see p. 106) to the passage of the First Crusade through the city in 1096/7.

THE
CRUSADES

109

All its main leaders, save one, took an oath of allegiance to the Emperor Alexius, but in truth their aims were incompatible. The eastern ruler did not want these large, inchoate bands of western knights inspired by their inextricable mixture of deep piety, lust for battle and land-hunger. If he had ever asked for anything, it was for compact bodies of mercenaries to defend and extend his own domains. The states established in Syria by the crusaders exacerbated the ecclesiastical disputes; for now Roman prelates were set up in cities like Antioch, which within living memory had been both Byzantine and orthodox. In Antioch itself reigned a dynasty from the tough, dominant Normans of south Italy who had been menacing Constantinople from the west for so long. It was from events of this sort, and from a waxing resentment against the commercial growth of Venice, that the hatred of Latins, or westerns, was engendered among the inhabitants of the Great City – inhabitants who still called themselves, to the astonishment of the crusaders, *Romaioi*, men of Rome.

On their side the crusaders began to feel a lack of sympathy with Constantinople. Their attitude was bellicose; they longed to slaughter infidels, they desired passionately to pray at the Holy Places, they had in most cases no objection to acquiring a fief on the way. They resented Byzantine advice, they disapproved of any diplomatic contact with Islam, forgetting that the Empire had now been a neighbour of divers Muslim powers for four centuries. During the Second Crusade Louis VII of France, who led his men with singular incompetence and neglect, had thought of assaulting Constantinople. During the Third Crusade, Barbarossa had menaced the Byzantine Emperor (England's Richard I, perhaps more prudently, went out by sea). How far there was a conspiracy behind the Fourth Crusade is still disputed, but the idea is plausible. When its organizers arrived in Venice, they were quite incapable of meeting the republic's bill for shipping. Starting with the minor impiety of a wanton attack upon the land of another Catholic crusader simply to suit Venice, the main body was easily lured by a Byzantine pretend/er and Venetian ambitions towards Constantinople. The prom/ises of claimants are more easily made than fulfilled, and in 1204 the irritated crusaders turned against their own puppet (Alexius IV). By this time they had formed a comprehensive idea of the riches of the capital city, both in material wealth and spiritual relics.

When the people of Constantinople also cast off the puppet emperor, total war broke out. The crusading host drew up in March a treaty dividing the future spoils among themselves. On 9 April the western Christians launched a full assault on the city, but it failed. Realizing that they had fallen short, they confessed and communicated, and dismissed all whores from their camp. In their effort to install the pretender, Alexius IV, the crusaders had already essayed the strength of the land walls in vain. Now they concentrated their vigour on the sea/walls of the Golden Horn. Alexius V, the new Emperor, had his head/quarters at the Pantepoptes to watch just this sector. The assault was launched on 12 April and after furious fighting the crusaders broke in, and established an enclave where they rested for that night. On the 13th Alexius V fled and resistance ceas/ed. For the first time the city of Constantine had fallen to an in/vader, not to the infidel or the heathen but to the self/styled sol/diers of Christ.

Plate 42

No serious distinction of dogma divided the adherents of the Pope, who fulminated frequently but tardily, from the followers of the Greek Church. None the less the crusaders flung them/selves into rape, rapine and pillage. Christian did not spare Christian. Nuns and nubile were alike ravished. In Hagia Sophia every fragment of silver was stripped from the ambo and the altar, while the sacred vessels were borne away as loot. 'Horses and mules were driven into the temple, and collapsed under their burdens so that their blood and ordure stained the floor.' Finally a young harlot, who had hastened to rejoin the ardent troops, sprang onto the altar and chanted a lewd ditty. 'O city, city, the eye of all cities, famous through all lands of the world, a vision out of this world, mother of churches, leader of faith, guide in orthodoxy, nurse of learning, why have you had to drink this cup of fury from the Lord,' lamented the contem-porary Nicetas Choniates. The reproaches were not one-sided: after the event, Pope Innocent III chided the crusaders for hav-ing spared neither the vows of religion, nor age, nor sex, and charged them with incest, adultery and fornication.

In particular the Great City was gutted of relics; nor were the jewelled reliquaries ignored. The treasury at Venice alone boasts 32 rich chalices. Soissons acquired the Veil of the Virgin and a head of St John Baptist. Louis of Blois secured for Char-tres the head of St Anne. Amiens gained another head of St John: did Greek instincts here outwit the gullible Frank? From the welter of spoliation, a stray English priest brought back to Bromholm a fragment of the True Cross. The fate of a similar morsel is unusually well documented: Constantine VII in about 959 caused to be fashioned an elaborate and superb re-liquary, perhaps the most splendid piece of craftsmanship by Byzantine goldsmiths and enamellers which has come down to us. It was acquired in 1204 by Heinrich von Ülmen, and can be traced from him to its present home at Limburg-an-der-Lahn. If the treasures of Christianity were plundered, those of antiquity were sacrificed, often to furnish the lower levels of coinage; the obelisk of Constantine VII in the Hippodrome was stripped, the famous bronze statues of Hera of Samos, of Hercules by Lysippus, of Paris giving the apple to Aphrodite were reduced to their base metal. Luckier were the four bronze horses in the Hippodrome, brought by Augustus to Rome from Alexandria, and by Constantine from Rome to his new city. Their journeying was not yet over; the Venetians bore them off to St Mark's, Napoleon swept them off to Paris and

Venice regained them after his fall. So efficient was the looting of the diligent crusaders that today it is easier to appreciate the minor arts of the great Byzantine period in Venice, or the Louvre, or Washington, D.C., than in Istanbul. The crusaders seem to have been uninterested in manuscripts.

Only the Venetians profited from the Fourth Crusade. Jerusalem gained no help, for all the high hopes of some of the participants. The Byzantine state, as we shall see, made a remarkable recovery, but was permanently and tragically enfeebled. The Latin Empire of Constantinople was frail, pitiful, discordant, not viable as a society. The papacy won no credit from its inability to control events. The defences of Europe against the Turk were gravely weakened, in the long run disastrously so. For the first time since 330, a crisis in the history of the city had failed to produce a Heraclius or a Leo to meet it.

In the dismemberment of the Empire carried out by the Fourth Crusade, the Latin Emperor, Baldwin of Flanders, got a quarter of the land. Venice acquired most of the best harbours; Greece was divided into feudal holdings. Constantinople itself was partitioned; five eighths went to Baldwin, and the rest to the open maw of the Venetians who were also exempted from any obligation to the Emperor. Three Byzantine succession states emerged from the chaos; in Asia Minor the Emperor Theodore I established himself at Nicaea, two other princes set themselves up, one in Epirus to the west and the other in distant Trebizond on the Black Sea.

Almost nothing survives, and little is known, of Latin government in the city itself. Baldwin and his successors lived mainly in the Blachernae Palace, which they left in a somewhat grimy condition. Some steps were taken to preserve Hagia Sophia (cf. p. 59), where a Venetian patriarch was installed. Most churches were converted to the Latin rite, but many of their relics and furnishings had already been shipped off to

France, Italy and Germany. Almost nothing was added to Constantinople by its Frankish conquerors, and a great deal was lost. One spectacular relic, the Crown of Thorns, had to be pawned to the Venetians, and finished up in the hands of St Louis, who built for it the Sainte Chapelle. The mosque of Arap Camii on the north side of the Golden Horn was proba/ bly first built in this period by the Dominicans, as the church of SS. Paul and Dominic. A severe fire in 1808 has not left much of the original structure.

Plate 44

In the summer of 1261, a Byzantine general was carrying out reconnaissance in Thrace. He found to his amazement that the capital was scantily protected and on 25 July he entered the city without difficulty. Baldwin II fled and on 15 August the Em/ peror Michael VIII (1259–82) entered by the Golden Gate and processed first to St John of Stoudios and then to Hagia Sophia where he was solemnly crowned a second time. His descendants were to reign until 1453, and the golden evening of Constantinople began.

THE
PALAEOLOGI

The empire of the Palaeologi was a very different affair from that of the Macedonian dynasty. Its territory was smaller, its manpower and resources more jejune. Their capital had been devastated and called for large sums in repair and redecoration, but the tax/paying provinces were fewer and less fertile than of old. A new dynasty was to revitalize the Turkish threat. None the less artistic patronage continued, though more of it was ex/ ercised by nobles and ministers than by the royal family, and new levels of achievement were realized. The lustrous period was in the first half of the fourteenth century.

Nothing was done on a large scale. Ever since the end of Iconoclasm the tendency had been for a sense of intimacy, and for smaller, and perhaps more numerous, churches. Monas/ teries had tended to decrease in size, unlike the great populous houses of the west; many Byzantine convents housed perhaps a dozen or twenty monks. Since the clergy increasingly occupied the naos (nave), there is a tendency to add accommodation in one or more narthexes. Much more care was lavished on the outside of churches and a fascinating skill in decorative brick-work was developed both in the capital and elsewhere. The ground plan tends to be governed by variations on the theme of a central dome imposed on a rectangle; within the rectangle will be nine linked sections – central space, choir, nave and transepts and the four corner areas between these five.

Naturally there are variations. The little church of St Mary of the Mongols has a unique plan and a romantic story. Erected for a bastard daughter of Michael VIII, who had been briefly wed to a Mongol khan, it has never ceased to be used for the orthodox liturgy. It was sadly damaged in a riot as late as 1955. Its plan is simple: the square dome compartment has on each side an apse, making the whole a quatrefoil. By tradition the Turkish conqueror assigned it to a Greek architect who had served him well. Not far from it is the present church of the Greek Patriarchate (the Phanar, see page 125 *infra*) which is quite modern.

Another unusual ground plan is that of Vefa Kilise Camii, usually identified with the church of St Theodore Tiro. Here the main body was built about 1100, but there was substantial reconstruction involving the narthex in the early fourteenth century. The outer narthex is capped by three domes in two of which are considerable traces of mosaic, though not of the first class. The brick decoration of the east end, probably belonging to the original church, is rich and varied, with recessed niches such as are found in the Comnenian age. At the west end, the later builders freely re-employed older materials, especially sculptured slabs, to lend variety to the façade; it is almost the technique which one must imagine as applied to the front of a secular palace, an idiom possibly borrowed from Constantinople by the oldest *palazzi* in Venice. Tucked away on a hillside,

Plate 43

Plate 45

near the south-east end of the aqueduct of Valens, this is an evocative building of great charm; it was transformed into a mosque by the tutor of the Conqueror.

More easily visible is Fethiye Camii, the former church of the Virgin Pammakaristos, the All Blessed. There was probably a monastery on this commanding position from the eleventh century, but the whole church was reconstructed in a splendid manner at the end of the thirteenth by Michael Glabas, and gives an excellent idea of a great private benefaction at this date. In plan it has a central dome-space with aisles on all sides but the east, not unlike the southern church of Lips(*cf.* p. 97) which is of just the same date. The dome has a high drum. Soon after the rebuilding, north and south aisles were added, and then in 1312 the widow of Glabas converted the south aisle into a chapel in memory of her husband. This delicious, miniature, and precisely dated parecclesion gains in lustre from a group of brilliant mosaics at the east end, which have recently been restored by the Americans. Only those in the dome were known before – Christ Pantokrator and 12 prophets; to these have been added a Baptism, sole survivor of the 'great feasts', Christ, the Virgin and St John in the apse and an interesting group of early bishops. Dating them is difficult: stylistic evolution was rapid in this spectacular period, and it seems easier to suppose that they were not executed until some years after the death of Glabas and are contemporary with the later work at Our Saviour in Chora. It should be added that the east end of the main church was altered and given a dome in Turkish times. Pammakaristos was the seat of the patriarchate from 1455 to 1586 and only then became a mosque. There is a crypt under the church.

Richest and most seductive of the Palaeologue churches is Our Saviour in Chora, a dedication which may allude to its remote position or to the place of Christ in our salvation. The problems of its early history may be ignored, for the whole was refashioned by Theodore Metochites between 1303 and 1326;

Plate 46

KARIYE
CAMII

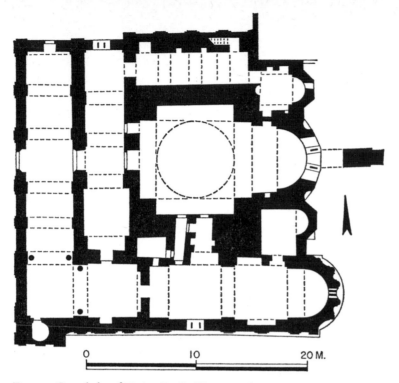

Fig. 20   Ground plan of Kariye Camii. AD 1303–26

in Turkish times it became a mosque as Kariye Camii, and since the war it has been cleaned and renovated by the devoted labours of Paul Underwood and the American Institute. The superb quality of the mosaics and the luminous marble panel‑ ling combine to make this perhaps the second most attractive Byzantine monument in the city, for all its barren secularization. Theodore himself is a sympathetic figure: statesman and author, his writings show clearly that he saw the impending doom which overhangs later Byzantium. After his death in 1331, as a monk, he was buried here in the southern parecclesion.

The plan is simple enough. A central dome covers a large crossing, with slight recesses for transepts, choir and nave – the

Plate 47

Fig. 20

117

pattern called 'atrophied Greek cross'. To the west are two large narthexes and to the south a mortuary chapel, with three smaller domes over them. The 'nave' has mosaics of considerable beauty including a fine Dormition; the series in the narthexes illustrates the life of the Virgin, and the early life and miracles of Christ. Even during the score or so of years which covered their execution there were stylistic changes, but the whole series is one of profound and moving beauty. It is invidious to single out special scenes, but the depiction of Theodore in his fantastic headgear offering his church (centre of esonarthex), the first tender steps of the Virgin, the brisk horsemanship of the Magi, the humour lurking in the Numbering of the People, all command attention. In the esonarthex too is a fine composition of the Virgin interceding with Christ, which also shows the princess Mary who espoused the Mongol *(cf.* p. 115). Parts are damaged and give a vivid opportunity to trace the successive layers of mosaic composition.

Equally striking, and of the same date, are the frescoes in the south parecclesion. It is instructive to recall that this makes these magnificent paintings contemporary with the work of Giotto at Padua. In the apse is the finest composition, an Anastasis, where the risen Lord with heroic vigour heaves Adam and Eve from Limbo and tramples Sin underfoot. No other frescoes of comparable value survive in the capital, though of course Byzantine influence and technique in this medium spread all through Greece and the Balkans and no doubt into Italy.

Fethiye Camii and Kariye Camii were the work of rich noblemen. One secular building has survived which must be associated with the Palaeologue period, the Tekfur Sarayı. This striking and still fairly well preserved ruin must be connected in some way with the Blachernae palace complex: but its precise place and date are undecided. Earlier generations linked it with Belisarius and Constantine VII, but the richness of the decora-

Plate 48

tion, the admixture of patterned brickwork and well-cut stone, strongly suggest an early fourteenth-century date. The actual structure is faintly suggestive of a western castle hall, as is the position absolutely against the city wall. It is tantalizing that this, the only substantial fragment of imperial palace architec-ture, splendid in its own way, should be so ill-documented and probably so untypical.

Plate 49

From such a vantage point the later emperors could look out over the undulating land to the west and contemplate their gradual encirclement by the Ottoman Turks. Passing years did not make the empire of the Palaeologues more robust; its scintil-lating artistic achievement was not matched in the harsher world of politics. The Black Death of 1347 removed perhaps a third of the shrinking population of the city. Fifteenth-century travellers – Clavijo, Buondelmonti, de Broquière – paint a gloomy picture of separated hamlets within the great walls, many churches in ruins and economic troubles. The great pal-ace was uninhabitable, mainly because Baldwin II had sold the lead off the roof. Many of the emperors, from Michael VIII on-wards, flirted with the idea of reunion with Rome; the concept was politically attractive, but won no sympathy or support from the ordinary people. It would be melancholy to trace in detail the fate of the various rulers. Manuel II travelled as far as the England of Henry IV in search of aid; but he was also compelled to become a vassal of the Sultan.

Around the year 1300 a minor Turkish leader named Osman had been growing in power south of the sea of Mar-mara. His son, Orhan, conquered Nicaea and crossed into Europe; furthermore, he built up a well-organized army. Or-han's son Murat I moved his headquarters from Brusa, in Asia, to Adrianople in 1365. Already Constantinople was, in the widest sense, beleaguered. John V in 1373 had to recognize the Sultan as overlord, like his son Manuel. In 1387 Salonika sur-rendered to Murat. Two years later his son Beyazıt I overwhelm-

THE
OTTOMANS

ed the Serbian kingdom at Kossovo, the Field of Blackbirds. In 1396 Beyazıt moved against Constantinople itself, but news came of a western crusade and he marched to rout it at Nicopolis; it was he who built Anadolu Hisarı, the castle dominating the Bosporos on the Asiatic side, but today somewhat ruined. For a while the immediate threat to the capital (and the Byzantine Empire now consisted of little more than Constantinople, a few islands and a province in the Peloponnese) was removed by the appearance of Tamurlane and his defeat of Beyazıt. In June 1422 Murat II mounted a full-scale assault on the walls of the Great City, but he lacked the siege artillery to breach them. The inhabitants again attributed their relief to the Virgin Mary. John VIII (1425–48), to judge by surviving inscriptions, did much to strengthen the walls; but he was repairing a medieval rampart and the atrocious modern weapon of gunpowder was now available. The defence in depth against artillery given by the walls of Rhodes, as reconstructed in the later fifteenth century, was never available to Constantinople. The year 1434 witnessed a terrible fire and 1440 an earthquake.

In 1449 Constantine XI succeeded to the throne of Constantine I: he was resolute and fearless, about forty-five years old. Two years later Mehmet II became Sultan. He had had a difficult childhood; now young (21), handsome and impetuous, he resolved on the conquest of the city. His first move was to build

Plates 50, 51

a great fortress on the European side of the Bosporos. Rumeli Hisarı was erected in four months. Older materials, Turkish and Byzantine, were ruthlessly re-employed. It cut off the city from Black Sea corn or any help from Trebizond; its three great towers and powerful curtain walls dominate the narrows and cannot easily be assaulted from land. Later legends attribute its irregular shape to the pattern of the letter M; more obviously it was a blatant threat to Constantinople.

The Emperor protested in vain. In 1439 the union of the Churches had been proclaimed at Florence, and he ventured to hope that this circumstance might be productive of aid. Instead of soldiers a cardinal arrived, and in December 1452 said mass in Hagia Sophia. The people were furious and one important minister, Lucas Notaras, uttered his famous cry that he preferred to see the Muslim turban rather than the Latin mitre within the city. All too soon his wish was fulfilled. That summer Constantine had been visited by a Hungarian cannon-founder called Urban, but he could not offer a sufficient stipend. The Magyar passed on to Mehmet and was given all that he desired in wages and materials.

On 7 April, 1453 the siege began. It has been described so vividly by Sir Steven Runciman that the tragic story need not be told in detail yet again. Save for a band of 700 Genoese led by the valiant Giovanni Giustiniani, the west was apathetic to this emergency of Christendom. On 20 April, the Byzantine forces won a naval battle but their joy was brief. Mehmet II had been unable to smash through the chain across the Golden Horn, but instead he transported his ships over the hill of Pera and into the harbour. The city was now completely invested. By day and night the bombardment by heavy guns went on: the defenders had but little artillery and that less effective.

The Sultan planned a great attack for May 29 and this was known within the city. On the evening of the 28th the notables and the captains attended a solemn service in Hagia Sophia, the last Christian liturgy, attended without rancour by orthodox and Latin alike. As the spring dusk fell, Constantine rode on his white-footed mare to the Great Church and prayed alone; then he returned to the walls. Early on the 29th the Turkish troops poured forward. From 1.30 a.m. to sunrise the struggle was furious. Then two tragedies occurred: Giustiniani was severely wounded, and a body of Turks got in through a sally port just below the Tekfur Sarayı. Constantine tried in vain to drive them out and then returned to the fifth military gate, in the Lycus valley where the barrage had been heaviest and the gaps widest. Discarding the imperial insignia, he dismounted and with three colleagues sought to stem the Janissaries as they poured in. He was never seen again, and it is doubtful if his body was ever identified. The last emperor had done all that valour and constancy could do. His resources were inadequate; he had deployed about 7,000 men bearing arms against 80,000 Turks, and he had sustained a siege of some seven weeks. The walls of the Prefect Anthemius had not been designed to resist the cannon of Urban.

CHAPTER VII

City of Minarets

Think, in this batter'd Caravanserai
Whose Portals are alternate Night and Day,
How Sultán after Sultán with his Pomp
Abode his destined Hour, and went his way.
　　　E. FITZGERALD, *Rubáiyát of Omar Khayyám,* XVII.

SO FELL CONSTANTINOPLE on Tuesday, 29 May.
Even today, no Greek will lightly select a Tuesday for an important function, a baptism or a wedding. The fatal attack broke through about dawn; it was not till the afternoon that the Conqueror (Fatih in Turkish) rode in to vaunt his new status. His route led to the great church of the Holy Wisdom, before which he dismounted; entering with humility he beheld a soldier hacking at the marble floor. Mehmet struck the man and announced that the church was reserved to himself. In a few moments Islam was proclaimed, and the Sultan prostrated himself on the altar stone to the glory of Allah. He then rode on to the Great Palace, now largely in ruins, and aptly quoted some Persian lines on the spider weaving curtains in the palace of the emperors. One pleasing tradition of Ayasofya, as it was henceforward called, asserts that as the last rite ended, some priests bearing their chalices miraculously passed into the south wall; thence they will not emerge until Christian worship takes place again in Hagia Sophia.

This conduct compared favourably with that of the Fourth Crusade. For the rest of Constantinople the end of May was grim. The army had been promised the three days of looting which were the prescribed doom of a city taken by assault. Indiscriminate slaughter, rape and plunder took place. Priests were murdered at the altar, nuns were ravished, libraries were burned, houses were sacked systematically and then marked with a pennant. The church of the Saviour in Chora, so near the walls, was an early victim. Hither had been taken the famous icon of the Virgin, painted by St Luke, which normally reposed in the convent of the Hodegetria, hard by the Great Church. Turkish troops paraded it through the town and then broke it in pieces. Lucas Notaras (see p. 121) soon regretted his epigram on turbans and mitres; he was executed after denying his boy to the Sultan's bed.

Mehmet now had to administer the burned and ruined city which had passed into his power. He had the wisdom to see that the solution lay in the Church. One of the most learned Byzantines of the age, George Scholarius, had entered religion under the name of Gennadius. The Conqueror caused him to be elected Patriarch, presented him with a new cross – the old one not being forthcoming – and gave him the church of the Holy Apostles for his see. Henceforward he and his successors were to be responsible to the sultans for the Christian and Greek population. Such a community was called a *millet* and was a traditional device of Islamic government. The patriarch was entitled to try ecclesiastical cases before his own tribunal, and was encouraged to set up civil courts for suits between Christians. Only direct crime brought them before the Turkish judges. This arrangement tended to knit the Greeks of Constantinople into a close community with a sense of survival; it tended also, in the capital and in Greece itself, to identify the Church with a historic sense of the imperial past and a living hope for a future, free of Turkish rule, which contributed to the Greek struggle for independence in the last century.

Gennadius did not stay long in Justinian's great church of the Apostles; it was already in poor condition, and in an area mainly Turkish. In 1455 he exchanged it for the monastery of Pammakaristos, nearer the Golden Horn, and standing above the part of Constantinople which was to become associated with the Greek community. A vanished lighthouse gave this quarter its name of the Phanar; and hence the epithet Phanariot was applied to the orthodox Christians of Constantinople. Rather curiously the Sultan and the Patriarch came to be on good terms, and Mehmet would discuss theology with Genna, dius in the parecclesion of the church. In 1586 Pammakaristos was seized by Murat III and became the mosque of Fethiye Camii. The patriarchate was transferred to the tiny church of St Demetrius and then to that of St George where it still exists; this church was rebuilt in 1720 and 1827, but still contains one fine Byzantine portable mosaic icon.

The Conqueror was resolved to make his new city into a worthy capital. He set about repairing the destruction of the conquest. Not only were his own compatriots encouraged to settle there, but Greeks were moved from Trebizond and were joined by Jews and Armenians; as prosperity and calm increas, ed, opportunity and stability beckoned all races to Constantin, ople in a manner impossible for two hundred years past. If a growth in population and commerce, and a splendid phase of building are to be the criteria, the last half of the fifteenth cent, ury was an age of prosperity for Constantinople. But by about 1500 most of the Christian churches had been turned into mos, ques. The process was haphazard and many of the conversions were executed by important Ottoman officials. For a generation or two it was easier to take over a Byzantine edifice than to build anew. Where this occurred the essentials of an Islamic place of worship had to be added to the Christian shrine. But a number of important mosques were also constructed in this period. The grand architectural process which gave Istanbul its present lovely skyline was under way.

It is an utter mistake to think of the Turks of 1453 as barbarians. The origins of the Ottoman family are obscure, and based upon Ghazi activity in Bithynia. The dynasty of Osman (of whose name Ottoman is a corruption) rose to power, however, upon

the verges of the reduced Byzantine empire; they had behind
them a long tradition of Islamic culture, even if they were hostile to its heirs. The Green Mosque in Brusa, their capital till
1413, and the Üşçerefeli Camii at Adrianople which was their
next centre, show clearly the sophistication and beauty of their
architecture before it was exposed to the influence of Byzantine
Constantinople.

MOSQUES   The purposes of a mosque are different from those of a church.
Congregational worship has small place in Islam. Every man
prays five times every day wherever he may be. A mosque is a
place of assembly where large congregations can listen to in-
struction or to the Koran, though of course any worshipper can
pray there if it is convenient. But the mid-day prayer on Friday
is said congregationally and a mosque must be big enough to
accommodate the men of the neighbourhood. A smaller place
of worship is styled a Mescid. (Incidentally, the courteous traveller will avoid both at noon on Fridays.) A fully equipped
mosque will normally have a cloistered courtyard with a fountain in the middle, for ablutions play a large part in Islamic
ritual. On the right of the entrance will be a minaret from the
balcony of which the muezzin utters his call to prayer. Within
the mosque must be a *minbar*, a staircased pulpit for sacred reading on Friday, and a preacher's chair, and above all the *mihrab*,
a niche pointing towards Mecca which determines the axis of
the whole building. If the mosque was built by a member of
the imperial family there may be two minarets, if by a sultan,
there are four. When the building has been converted from a
church, which normally faces east, the *mihrab* will be at an angle
to the main axis.

See Plate 3   In 1463 the Conqueror began the great mosque which still
bears his name on the site of the church of the Holy Apostles
which was therefore demolished. The mosque was brought
down by an earthquake in 1766 and we do not know details of
its construction, but it seems to have been in the tradition of

earlier Muslim architecture and to have owed nothing to Byzantine ideas. The rebuilding lacked distinction and produced
a conventional domed space which is not really worthy of its
superb site. Other early mosques echo the technique of Brusa.
That of Murat Paşa (about 1470) is perhaps the best example.
The ground plan is shaped like a T. A broad vestibule with
small cupolas, leads into a prayer-hall with two domes, but
the first, flanked with smaller cells, is noticeably broader than
the more southerly which contains the *mihrab*. Another charming little mosque, Atik Ali Paşa Camii, near the Burned Column, was founded in 1496 and has an even simpler T shape;
this is thought to echo the ground plan of the original Fatih.
While Murat Paşa built his mosque in alternate courses of
brick and stone, Atik Ali Paşa used only stone. Although the
Turks, naturally enough, continued to employ a lot of brickwork, they turned increasingly to stone for their formal or elaborate buildings.

The first need of the Conqueror was a palace. Neither the
ruins of the Great Palace, nor the later Blachernae Palace attracted him. Accordingly he built a new abode on the site of
the forum of Theodosius, more or less where the University
now stands. The Eski Saray (old palace), as it came to be
known, was begun in 1454, but was soon replaced and has
now vanished completely. At the same time Mehmet required
a strong point, and in 1457 he began an extensive fortification
by the Golden Gate. Using the Theodosian wall on one side,
he added an enceinte on the city side which eventually came to
have the seven towers which give its Turkish name of Yedikule Hisarı. This fortress guarded the approach from the west and
may have served initially as a repository for the treasures of
state: soon however it became a prison and one Sultan (Osman
II in 1622) was strangled here. Four of the towers were Byzantine, though two of them were virtually rebuilt after an earthquake in 1750, and the three townward ones were Turkish. As

Fig. 21

Plate 52

Plate 53

at the slightly earlier Rumeli Hisarı, there was once a mosque in the centre. The idea was not a new one, for there had been a less elaborate Byzantine strong-point here. The towers originally had conical caps.

THE SARAY These enterprises were both put in the shade by the imperial residence which was begun in 1472–8 on the site of the original acropolis of Byzantium. At first it was called the New Palace (Sarayı cedit), and then, when newer palaces still were con-structed along the shores of the Bosporos, it became known as Topkapı Sarayı (literally Cannon Gate Palace; a title which can cause confusion since one of the gates in the Theodosian wall has the same name), or even as the Old Palace. This enormous complex covers an area of some 700,000 square me-tres and has been altered or adapted by almost every sultan. The whole area was surrounded by a defensive wall, never in the event seriously tested, running from the mouth of the Golden Horn almost to Hagia Sophia, passing between that church and Hagia Eirene (which is within the compound) and down to the sea. The wall thus encloses a quantity of lower ground, including the Mangana quarter of the Byzantines, but the Turkish palace is mainly concentrated on the hill-top.

Within these walls lived and moved, intrigued and loved and wept, an entire small town. The kitchens, built by the great Sinan in the sixteenth century, were geared to feed 5,000 per-sons a day and 10,000 on holidays. Scattered around the vast enclosure were ten mosques, fourteen baths and two hospitals; 4,000 horses occupied the stables.

It would be impossible to describe the Saray in detail; so many reigns and cultures are mingled here, that a few general impressions must suffice. It is an open site, rather as a Byzan-tine palace must have been, but can be regarded as a series of courts, each narrower than the last, moving from south-west to north-east. The normal entrance was by the Bâbı-Humayun, close to Hagia Sophia and to a decorative fountain erected by Sultan Ahmet III; this was the main approach for the sultans themselves, for ambassadors and for visitors of importance. Within is a large grassy enclosure, dominated on the left by the church of Hagia Eirene, still surrounded by cannons and culverins. Past Hagia Eirene a path leads down to the Museums – the Hittite Museum and the richly endowed Museum of Archaeology, replete with Hellenistic and Byzantine treasures. Between the two, and devoted to relics of the Conqueror, is the Çinili Kiosk, or Pavilion of Tiles, an elegant structure put up by Mehmet II; it is gaily decorated with encaustic tiles of an early pattern, and possesses a light loggia of arches borne by slender columns.

The first courtyard of the Saray leads the traveller on to the Ortakapı (Middle Gate) where nowadays he pays for his admission. Under the open space are the remains of a Byzantine basilica; and in a little yard to the right can be seen a gigantic capital, which probably once graced the summit of a late Roman column, and a sarcophagus. Also on the right is the noble range of kitchens, now given over to a magnificent collection of oriental porcelain. It is a sad reflection on the later sultans that the wonderful series of celadon pottery was found, after their fall, still enclosed in the original packing cases from China. On the other side of the quadrangle is a tall tower, a landmark in the city's skyline, whose lower story belongs to the Conqueror, though the summit is three hundred years later. The central path of the second court leads to the Gate of Felicity (Bâb-üs-saade) through which the third court is entered; the grouping of the buildings now becomes more haphazard, dependent on the fancy of sultan after sultan. Immediately in front is the Hall of Audiences, an early building restored in later years but still boasting fine ceramic work. To the right are a chain of apartments housing the treasures of the sultans, almost glaring in their opulence of gold and jewelry. The last room, the ancient

Plate 26

treasury, belongs to the first age of the palace and opens on to a welcome terrace with a noble panorama of the Bosporos and the Sea of Marmara. On the left of the third court, behind a small mosque of fifteenth-century date now converted into a library, is the beginning of the extensive harem area. The entrance is inconspicuous and the warren within, constructed on several levels, contains about 250 rooms of various sizes. Almost all were redecorated or reconstructed after a fire in 1663,

Plate 55

but noteworthy tiles of an earlier age survive. Romance has played around the seraglio, but in truth the emotions here must have been of boredom and intrigue, of frustration and jealousy, among the charming and chattering competitors for the favour of a night. The harem as a whole was not moved to this palace from the Eski Saray until about 1550. At some moments the harem contained nearly 2,000 women and girls in various stages of training; it is however noticeable that those who attracted the attentions of the ruler and bore children were scarcely ever Turkish. By male descent the later sultans were no doubt derived from Osman I (d. 1326) but the percentage of actual Turkish blood in their veins was negligible.

The north-east end of the Saray displays some of its loveliest features, and on all sides terraces give views over Constantinople and Pera. In the furthest corner, looking over a sunken garden, is the Baghdad Kiosk, built in 1638 to commemorate a victory there by Murat IV (1623–40). Every finesse of Turkish lightness of design, superb faience panelling, mother-of-pearl inlay and a bronze chimney-piece unite to charm the eye. Across the courtyard is another pavilion, the Erivan Kiosk (1635) recalling another victory; again the tiles are lovely but the whole effect is less dazzling. A later phase of Ottoman art is represented by the wooden pavilion of Mustafa Paşa restored in 1704 by Ahmet III and later repaired in 1752 by Mahmut I.

In 1517 Sultan Selim I waged war in Egypt and his artillery prevailed over the dash of Mameluke horsemen; the campaign degenerated into a sorry series of reprisals on prisoners and envoys. The last Mameluke Sultan was hanged before the gates of Cairo and Selim brought back to Turkey the precious relics of the Prophet and the title of Caliph of Islam. Portions of the beard of Muhammad, his sword, staff, seal and mantle were installed in the Saray. The chambers which house them were reconstructed in the eighteenth century by Mahmut I. The banner of the Prophet was brought from Damascus to join them in 1595. The actual objects are housed in rich coffers and are venerated by all Muslims. Other rich collections of manuscripts, of robes, of armour and of pictures (for the sultans were some, times prepared to evade the laws against wine and human por, traits) combine to give some idea of the splendour of the Otto, man court. None the less the whole Saray has an empty look, and occasional parties of visitors fail to reproduce the pulsing, thronging life of its heyday.

Plate 56

The advent of the Turks did not protect Constantinople from natural or civil disasters. The succession of Beyazıt II (1481– 1512) to the Conqueror was disputed, and the troops of his brother forced an entry into the city and pillaged part of it. In 1509 a serious earthquake damaged the new mosque of the Fatih and many older buildings; among them was the gate of Jesus (Isa Kapousı) where the Mēsē crossed the Constantinian wall.

The first of the great imperial mosques was built in 1501–5 by Beyazıt II on the edge of the forum of Theodosius and near the now vanished Eski Saray. This site has been a centre of communications and traffic from the age of Theodosius to to, day. By this date the Turks had had opportunity to study and admire Hagia Sophia which had become their grandest mos, que. The ground plan is a compromise between two traditions; in the actual mosque the dome and two, half, domes of Hagia Sophia are repeated but the whole design becomes squarer and

Plate 57

Fig. 21   The main Turkish monuments of Constantinople

lmabahçe
lace

2

B-O-S-P-O-R-O-S

1   Piyalepaşa Camii
2   Sinan Paşa Camii
3   Kariye Camii
4   Fethiye Camii
5   Selimiye Camii
6   Gül Camii
7   Azapkapısı Camii
8   Kılıç Ali Paşa Camii
9   Mihrümah Camii
10 Fatih Camii Complex
11 Fenari İsa Camii
12 Şehzade Camii
13 Burmali Minare Mescidi
14 Süleymaniye Camii Complex
15 Rüstem Paşa Camii
16 Yeni Camii
17 Archaeological Museum
18 Ayasofya Museum
19 Sultan Ahmet Camii (Blue Mosque)
20 Mosaic Museum
21 Küçük Ayasofya Camii
22 Sokollu Mehmet Paşa Camii
23 Atik Ali Paşa Camii
24 Burned Column
25 Nurosmaniye Camii
26 Beyazıt Camii
27 Bath of Beyazıt
28 Laleli Camii
29 Aksaray Camii
30 Murat Paşa Camii
31 Cerrahpaşa Camii
32 Hekimoğlu Ali Paşa Camii
33 Ramazan Efendi Camii
34 Koca Mustafa Paşa Camii
35 İmrahor Camii
A   Golden Gate
B   Topkapı Gate
C   Adrianople Gate
D   Cibali Gate

Note: Camii = Mosque

-H.A.S-

133

the aisles are clearly incorporated in the main scheme. On the other hand the half-dome nearer to the great entry porch is flanked by two wings which protrude to right and left beyond the mosque and its courtyard and preserve something of the older inverted-T form. One of the minarets still has its original polychrome decoration. The architect is said to be Hayrettin: if so, he successfully appropriated and adapted Byzantine ideas to Turkish needs and achieved something new in the process.

The next ruler, Selim I (1512–20), chose a site in the north of the city near the Golden Horn. The impressive Sultan Selim Camii was a more conservative building with a large domed central space, adjoined by two smaller units and a portico – the T upside down in its basic simplicity. The internal decoration is lavish and has been little altered in later centuries. In its slightly remote and lofty position it makes a striking contribution to the skyline, but is not often visited.

SINAN AND
SÜLEYMAN

The reign of Süleyman I (1520–66) brings on to the stage one the world's finest and most inventive, and perhaps most neglected architects, the great Sinan. This remarkable man was born about 1491 and died in 1588: this means that by the Islamic calendar, with its shorter year, he was over 100 years old. He was probably born in Albania, but the whole of his early career is shrouded in uncertainty. It is known that he became a Janissary and fought at Rhodes and Belgrade; he became a military engineer but only turned to large-scale architecture when he was about 50. Eighty full-scale mosques, fifty of the smaller prayer houses of the kind called a Mescid, schools, kitchens, bridges, aqueducts, palaces and baths all over Turkey attest his versatility and his capacity for fresh designs within a restricted formula.

He was happy in his principal patron, for Sultan Süleyman, the Magnificent to western narrators but the Lawgiver to his own people, was a brilliant ruler, cultivated and successful, though as capable as all his dynasty of moments of demoniac cruelty. From Rhodes to Hungary his armies were triumphant and new provinces paid their taxes to his treasury and their tribute of children to his Janissaries. In his reign Sinan constructed three great mosques for members of the dynasty. A favourite son of the Sultan had died in 1543 and the Mosque of the Prince (Şehzade Camii) was his memorial. It has a noble setting: on one side runs the great road to Edirne (Adrianople), on the other begins the aqueduct of Valens. The building is of great beauty and is an astonishing creation for an architect who had apparently never tackled a major work before. The central dome is buttressed on all four sides by half-domes, itself a striking new development, but it is the harmony and simple probity of the proportions which give pleasure. Both minarets are richly decorated, and there are a number of royal tombs (*türbe*) in the compound: they are embellished with tiles but rarely open. The cannelures of the main columns of the mosque suggest that Sinan's attentive eye may have observed a classical model.

Şehzade was finished in 1548. At the same period Sinan was building, next to the wall by the Adrianople gate, a mosque for Princess Mihrümah, a sister of the dead prince and married to the formidable and unsmiling Rüstem Paşa, the Grand Vizier. The dates are not established, but Egli, the biographer of Sinan, suggests 1540–50. Here again the architect propounds a new solution to the problem of covering a large space; he abolishes the half-domes altogether and contrives to make the four walls support the central dome with no help other than four fairly massive corner turrets behind the squinches.

The third imperial mosque and the noblest was built for the Sultan himself. More than any other building in the capital the Süleymaniye Camii stands as an example of lavish good works and superb design. The actual mosque is the centre of an extensive group of ancillary buildings and dominates not only them, but the hill and a wide area of the city. Four schools, a training college, a library, a bath, a hospital, a public kitchen to feed worshippers and a hostel to lodge them, an asylum and a

Plate 58

lodge for the guardian of the tombs were added by the Sultan to his benefaction. He and his favourite wife, Roxelana, have each their own *türbe,* and in a corner by the precinct lies Sinan himself. Most of the adjacent buildings have now been convert-ed into libraries or museums. It was normal for a large mosque to have some of these dependencies, especially a hostel and kitchen (*imaret*), but not on this scale.

It has been suggested that Sinan had been experimenting with alternative solutions to the plan of Hagia Sophia and now came back to the Byzantine lay-out. Certainly we see again a great dome between two half-domes, and an extensive rectan-gular fore-court, but the handling of these features produces a building of a quite different character. Perhaps Sinan was deliberately accepting the challenge of the older masterpiece, resolved to translate its language into a paean of his own. He relies on proportion for his bold effects, hardly employing tiles at all, though there is good stained glass above the *mihrab,* the work of Ibrahim Sarhoş (the drunkard). The interior has re-cently been repainted, and after some years of scaffolding, one can see again how light penetrates into every corner of the build-ing. Here is no sense of mystery, but a noble hall of prayer crowned by a dome which is the natural summit of the great stone building. The thrust of the dome is unostentatiously met by buttresses within the walls and at the north end by piers supporting the gallery. Only on the south exterior wall is one conscious of the scale of the buttressing required. The dome itself is 26.5 m. across and 53 m. high.

During its construction (1550–7) Sinan made consider-able use of existing materials. The splendid courtyard at the west end is surrounded by porticos with 28 cupolas; almost all the columns of the porticos are re-used from Byzantine and other sites. Within the mosque the tympana to north and south, a fairly direct borrowing from Hagia Sophia, are carried on four monolithic columns; two came from Baalbek and Alex-

Fig. 22

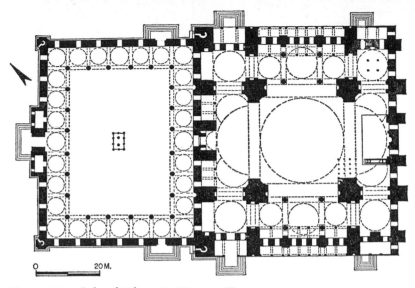

Fig. 22   Ground plan of Süleymaniye Mosque. AD 1550–7

andria, and a third from the Great Palace, while the fourth
(which had to be shortened) was a famous pillar of the Virgin-
ity which stood near the Holy Apostles on the fifth hill. This
may once have supported a statue of Constantine. (An earlier
column of the same name stood on the third hill with a statue
of Aphrodite alleged to indicate those who had lost their chas-
tity: a kinswoman of Justin I caused it to be destroyed rather
than pass by.) The inscriptions inside the mosque are the work
of Hassan Çelebi, a master of writing. The acoustics are admirable. But one should not ignore the outside: the arrangement of
the exterior masses achieves a far more rhythmic ascent to the
final dome than the much altered exterior of Hagia Sophia.
Four minarets spring from the corners of the fore-court: by
tradition the number indicates that Süleyman was the fourth
sultan since the conquest, while the ten balconies round them
proclaim that he was tenth in lineage from Osman I. This was
the first mosque with four minarets, though the number was

repeated in the even more beautiful one built in Edirne (Adrianople) by Sinan for Selim II.

The great architect created a large number of smaller mosques in Constantinople (and elsewhere), and was equally fertile in experiment on a less grandiose scale. One of the most rewarding is that of Rüstem Paşa the husband of Princess Mihrümah, which stands on the first floor since it is in a very busy shopping quarter, and was begun in 1561. Here the main dome is carried on four pillars and four charming small half-domes, where a Byzantine architect might have put pendentives. It is an interior of extreme elegance, but the eye is distracted by the ravishing beauty of the Nicene tiles which cover all the walls and repeat their fresh and vivid floral patterns with enough variety to prevent the least suggestion of monotony. The production of this delightful aid to interior décor is one of the triumphs of Turkish arts in this period. Early in the sixteenth century Selim I had installed whole families of ceramic craftsmen from Persia at Nicaea, now known as Iznik, and the finest tiles came from this region. A high standard of production, colour and design was maintained for the rest of that century but fell off in the seventeenth. Early in the eighteenth century a group of potters established themselves in the Tekfur Sarayı (see p. 118) but their work, attractive enough by other standards, falls below the best tiles of the great age.

Sinan was constantly concerned with the supports of the dome. Esmahan, daughter of Selim II and wife of another Grand Vizier, Sokollu Mehmet Paşa, desired to found a mosque on the hillside just above the church of SS. Sergius and Bacchus. The site was a difficult one, but Sinan contrived, in about 1571, an ingenious and satisfying solution; the dome is borne by a hexagon of which the four lateral sides are buttressed by little half-domes. The *mihrab* wall is faced with tiles of the best period and all the interior fittings are of the highest quality. Elements of the ground plan can be found in a pre-conquest

Plate 59

mosque in Edirne, but once again the architect has transmuted precedent into a building which bears the hall-mark of his own genius.

He was also responsible for at least another thirty mosques in Constantinople and its suburbs. Some were very humble. The mosque now called Ramazan Efendi Camii which can be dated to the end of his life (1586) is small, and of too modest a donor to rate a dome, but the interior is brilliant with the best Nicene tiles. Its simple rectangular plan with a square, pitched roof, can be paralleled in the Mescid called Burmalı Minare adjacent to the Şehzade; the architect is unknown but he devised here a striking minaret with a spiral brick pattern.

Three mosques at least on the Galata side of the Golden Horn deserve brief mention in any appraisal of Sinan. That of Piyale Paşa, Grand Admiral and another son-in-law of Selim II – for the daughters of sultans, a superfluous class, were often bestowed on the dignitaries of the court – is remote but interesting, for it recalls the earliest Asian mosques; the hall of prayer (1573) is divided into six compartments, each with its own cupola; the minaret, unusually, is in the middle of the façade. Long ago the site was connected with the Golden Horn by a canal; and it is perhaps not over-fanciful to detect a vaguely ship-like appearance in the whole structure; on the other hand Sinan may have been recuperating intellectually by returning to an old traditional pattern. Similarly, perhaps, in the Mosque of Azapkapısı (1577) just by the western bridge across the Golden Horn, he reverts to the same basic plan as he had employed in Rüstem Paşa; here again the building is well above ground level; it was ordered by the Grand Vizier Sokollu, but has suffered more from time and the restorer than either Sokollu's name-mosque or that of Rüstem.

Kılıç Ali Paşa was another admiral and commanded a mosque on the Bosporos side of Galata. Sinan erected this for him in 1580, when he must have been about 90. Possibly from

Plate 60
Plate 61

Plate 62

Plate 63

affection, he went back to the plan of Sülemaniye (and behind it that of Beyazıt and Hagia Sophia). An elaborate porch with five cupolas leads into a dominating interior, where the prolong-ation of the galleries along the whole length of both aisles and a small extension at the Mecca end conjure up a comparison with one of the city churches of Christopher Wren, whose life and problems had so much in common with those of Sinan. Finally one might mention an earlier experiment, the mosque of the Admiral Sinan Paşa built in 1555 by the architect Sinan, who was no relation at all; here the outside is an attractive pat-tern of horizontal brick and stone courses and the interior is a variant on the hexagonal theme. Wren and Sinan both worked in an age of golden opportunity; both had to ring the changes on a basic theme which gave only limited opportunities for variety; both nobly seized their chances.

The descendants of Süleyman were less able and less successful, though they continued to be patrons of the arts. Selim II, known as the Sot, had a passion for wine and abrogated the law against its consumption. The Turkish naval defeat of Lepanto by that romantic leader, Don John of Austria (1571), took place in his reign, but was not of great significance in the long run. His son, Murat III (1574–95), was a great lover of women and considerably enlarged the harem quarters of the New Saray. He also gave a cordial welcome to William Har-borne, the first English emissary to Constantinople, who organ-ised the Turkey Company there in 1579. France was already well established, for an alliance between her king and the sultan had been arranged in 1535, to the horror of Catholic Christen-dom. Like the Byzantine Emperor Theophilus, Murat liked to perambulate his capital by night, and hear the complaints of his subjects; though avaricious, he gave splendid feasts, and it is the portrayal of the grand celebrations for the circumcision of his son which depicts the Delphic column (cf. p. 27).

Ever since the days of the Conqueror the cruel law of fratricide had prevailed, whereby a new sultan, on his succession, put to death all his brothers to avoid possibility of dispute or civil war; the loss of a prince or two was less to be deplored than that of a province, and indeed the Ottoman Empire was noticeably free of internal strife. At the death of Murat, his son Mehmet III consigned no less than nineteen brothers to be strangled by mutes with a silken bow-string, the most honourable form of death. On several occasions this left the sultan as the only male descendant of Osman, but the resources of the harem were always sufficiently varied to provide an heir. Gradually in the seventeenth century the practice changed to the confinement of cadets of the dynasty within the Saray, where, in the fourth court, were a series of the pavilions known as Kafes. On too many occasions a bemused or inexperienced prince had to be released from the Kafes to assume the throne of a dead brother.

Another disquieting feature was the growing power of the corps of Janissaries. These regiments of pride had originally been recruited from Christian children, trained and brought up in Islam and vowed to celibacy and the sultan's service. By the seventeenth century they had taken to marriage and aped many of the worst features of the later Roman army. Every incoming sultan was obliged to reward them with a bonus and many of the fleeting rulers of the period were set up or put down by the intransigent and undisciplined soldiery. Mustafa I, who was half-witted, was twice thus dragged to the throne.

Mehmet III received one splendid present, an organ brought from England and installed by Thomas Dallam, a member of a distinguished family of organ-builders who left a most amusing account of his experiences. On the top of the instrument was a holly bush, full of blackbirds and thrushes which sang and shook their wings. The ghost of Theophilus must have smiled. Mehmet offered Dallam two concubines at his choice if he would stay in Constantinople.

Plate 66

Mehmet's mother was responsible for another large-scale mosque. The Yeni (New) Cami stands at the south end of the Galata bridge and is seen by everybody, examined perhaps by fewer. Safiye began it in 1597, but first the architect died and then, in 1603, her son. This deprived her of power, and the building remained unfinished until the mother of Mehmet IV ordered Mustafa Ağa to complete it, which was achieved in 1663. The outside is a well-balanced composition, rising skilfully to a large dome: within, this can be seen to be based on four half-domes (like Sinan's mosque of Şehzade), with smaller cupolas in the corners. The decoration is of late, but pleasant, faience including a striking frieze-inscription in ceramic.

THE BLUE
MOSQUE

In the interval between the start and finish of the New Mosque, a more ambitious project was undertaken by the otherwise unmemorable Sultan Ahmet I (1603–17). Politically his reign marked a decline in Turkish power, and by the Treaty of Torok (1606) Austria ceased to pay the humiliating tribute of 30,000 ducats imposed by Süleyman I, but he left behind him a splendid memorial. Choosing as a site the remains, doubtless by now hopelessly decayed, of the Byzantine Great Palace and its access to the Hippodrome he raised the last great imperial mosque between 1609 and 1617. The architect was Sedefkâr Mehmet Ağa and the whole complex was on a magnificent scale. The exterior is a most splendid and successful concept: nowhere are the

Plate 64

pyramidic possibilities of a series of rising curves more ingeniously and satisfactorily exploited. The effect is enhanced by the advantages of the open site and by the innovation of six minarets, four at the corners of the building and two more at the outer angles of the imposing court-yard. The legend that Ahmet had to placate the guardians of Mecca is without foundation; the mosque there already boasted seven minarets.

Within, the decoration is exceedingly rich: 20,000 tiles were used, including among their floral patterns no less than 50 variations on the tulip theme. But a note of azure predominates

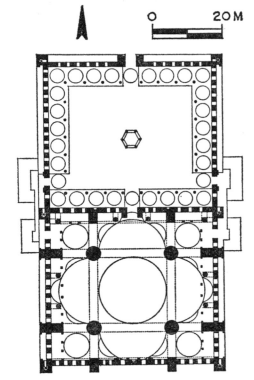

O   20 M

Fig. 23 Ground plan of
Mosque of Sultan Ahmet
(the 'Blue Mosque').
AD 1609–17

and is continued in the frescoed patterns above pillar height;
hence comes the common title of the 'Blue Mosque'. Architec-
turally the plan is bold and majestic. Once again the great dome
(43 m. high and 23.5 m. across – still less than that of Hagia
Sophia) is buttressed by four half-domes and the whole ground   Fig. 23
plan is based upon a perfect square. Much of the weight of the
dome is carried on four enormous fluted columns, 5 m. in diameter, and they appear to labour a little under their burden. It is
impossible to deny that the over-all effect is impressive, but the   Plate 65
precise symmetry may not be a complete advantage, and the
subtlety which is inherent in Hagia Sophia and in the Süleymaniye mosque is a little lacking here. In fact, only in Sinan's

masterpiece at Edirne did Turkish architects achieve a dome higher or wider than that of Anthemius a thousand years before. None the less, the Blue Mosque with its family of elegant mina/ rets has its own contribution to make to the skyline.

In politics and architecture the story of Constantinople contin/ ued to be one of ups and downs. In 1612 the Dutch made a com/ mercial treaty and were seemingly responsible for the introduc/ tion of tobacco to the Ottoman Empire. Plagues occurred, par/ ticularly in 1626. The Janissaries went on giving trouble till they were abolished early in the nineteenth century. Fires were frequent and formidable, for if the great mosques were of stone, the houses of the poor and of the fairly rich also were of wood,

Plate 67

and were packed together in dangerous neighbourhood. The same was true of the growing suburb on the north side of the Golden Horn. Even today this area is dominated by the Galata tower, almost an epitome of the history of the city. The masonry at its base is itself certainly early Byzantine, but even before 1204 the tower appears to have been incorporated in the Geno/ ese fortifications of their quarter at Galata, and they rebuilt the

See Plate 62

upper part in about 1350. The Turks reduced the height under the Conqueror, and then converted the top story into a post for fire/watching. At the moment of writing it is again under/ going reconstruction.

Buildings of distinction continued to be erected in what may by now be called the Turkish classical style. Perhaps the last of them is the fine mosque of Hekimoğlu Ali Paşa built in 1732–4 on a hexagonal plan, related to Sinan's Sokollu mosque. The widespread display of tiles within represents a good sample of the ceramic workers of the Tekfur Sarayı. Of the same date is

Plate 54

the handsome fountain of Tophane, next door to the mosque of Kılıç Ali Paşa: here the elaborate carvings in low relief have a flavour of those on the Taj Mahal at Agra. But inch by inch western culture invaded the sphere of Turkish art. In 1748 the

Nuruosmaniye Camii shows a clear infiltration of baroque. In the nineteenth century the series of great palaces along the Bosporos are emphatically European in feeling. In 1854 the mosque of Ortaköy, also on the Bosporos, uses Corinthian columns and capitals for its slender minarets and their balconies. The effect is graceful enough, but it has ceased to be Turkish. The extreme of imitative indigestion is reached in the mosque of Aksaray (1871), designed by an Italian who may charitably be supposed to have begun life as a pastrycook.

CHAPTER VIII

Epilogue

The cloud-capp'd towers, the gorgeous palaces
The solemn temples...

        ...shall dissolve.

        SHAKESPEARE, *Tempest* IV I

As WILL HAVE BEEN SEEN, Constantinople has been many things: the capital and centre of the East Roman or Byzantine Empire for over a millennium, the head of a struggling Latin state for five decades, the capital of the Turkish Sultanate for nearly five centuries. To the Russians it was Tsarigrad the town of Caesar; the Norsemen and Varangians named it Micklegarth. As the Ottoman dynasty declined politically – and as late as 1683 it was besieging Vienna – the city became increasingly cosmopolitan. A large, and on the whole ugly, European residential and shopping quarter grew up on the high land to the north of the Golden Horn. Houses spread on the eastern shore of the Bosporos in Üsküdar and Kadiköy. In the former (though she knew it as Scutari) Miss Nightingale had her hospital. Today more than a hundred thousand intercontinental commuters cross daily from Asia to work in Istanbul.

How this name arose for the imperial city is something of a problem. The form Astanbul occurs as early as Ibn Batuta, writing Arabic in 1350 or so. This makes less likely the widely accepted view that Istanbul is a Turkish version of the Greek words 'in the city' (eis tēn polin). In the west the form Stamboul was current, but it is not easy for Turks to pronounce two initial consonants; Istanbul is possibly therefore neither more nor less than a failure to pronounce Constantinoupolis in all its syllables. The hazards of the epithet 'Constantinopolitan' may account for the popularity of 'Byzantine'.

During the nineteenth century the Great City and the Bosporus figured constantly in international politics because of

Russian ambitions both for Constantinople, the great cradle of the orthodox faith, and also for an ice-free access to her ports. In 1923 came the severest blow of all, when the National Assembly decreed that henceforward Ankara would be the capital of Turkey. The proud city of Constantine and Justinian, of Sinan and Süleyman sank from the first place for the first time.

It is not the end. Changes continue: broad boulevards are driven through the city, leaving the antiquary with a haunting curiosity as to what may lie beneath them. Traffic pullulates through the narrower streets of Sirkeci and Galata. The liberal policy of Atatürk has allowed the restoration of the mosaics, and the opening of more and more sections of the Saray. The double heritage of Byzantium and Islam is a heavy burden on the available resources, although a double attraction to the traveller and the historian. The Golden Horn, once chain-protected, is now spanned by two bridges; the railway has made havoc of sections of the sea-wall and the Mangana Palace; trams grind up the acropolis to Hagia Sophia; and a delightful 'underground' travels uphill from Galata to Beyoğlu. Yet the walls still confront the air passenger from Yesilköy; the fortunate seafarer beholds the varied line of minarets at dawn before the smoke has begun to rise from the steamers; obscure and hidden remnants of all the generations which have gone to build the city still wait to be discovered. There may be a certain melancholy in Constantinople, the regrets of widowhood and great age, but there is also a store of beauty, of history, of memories long sustained, of romance, tragedy, brutality, and heroism which are part of the story of mankind. No European can withhold gratitude from this venerable and potent fortress, the guardian of religion and learning, when the infant culture of western Christendom was slowly moving towards the appreciation and apprehension of such things. In some sense, we have all sheltered behind the walls of Constantinople.

Bibliography

There is an extensive, and ever-growing, literature on the Byzantine world and, directly or indirectly, on its chief city. The following list is intended as a brief guide to further reading; it only includes relatively recent books.

GENERAL HISTORY

OSTROGORSKY, G., *History of the Byzantine State*. (Translated by Joan Hussey.) Oxford 1956. A masterly survey of Byzantine history by the most distinguished living Byzantine historian. Includes extensive bibliographies; a new English edition is in preparation.

BAYNES, N. H., *The Byzantine Empire*. Oxford 1926.

HUSSEY, J. M., *The Byzantine World*. London 1957.
Two admirable short introductory studies.

ART AND CIVILISATION

BAYNES, N. H., and MOSS, H. St L. B. *Byzantium*. Oxford 1948. An introductory symposium by various hands: illustrated.

RUNCIMAN, SIR STEVEN, *Byzantine Civilisation*. London 1933.

DIEHL, CHARLES, *Byzantium: Greatness and Decline*. (Translated by Naomi Walford.) New Brunswick 1957. A lively introduction.

RICE, DAVID TALBOT, *The Art of Byzantium*. Photographs by Max Hirmer. London 1959. A splendidly illustrated survey of the art of the Byzantine Empire, based in the first instance on the excellent exhibition held in Edinburgh and London in 1958.

BECKWITH, JOHN, *The Art of Constantinople*. London 1961.

KRAUTHEIMER, RICHARD, *Early Christian and Byzantine Architecture*, Harmondsworth 1965. A wide and authoritative survey, with an extensive bibliography of recent work in the notes.

MATHEW, GERVASE, *Byzantine Aesthetics*. London 1963.

HAMILTON, J. A., *Byzantine Architecture and Decoration*. Revised edition, London 1956. A useful survey.

RICE, DAVID TALBOT, *The Byzantines*. Revised impression London 1964. Describes the Byzantine people and their culture.

THE CITY

LIDDELL, ROBERT, *Byzantium and Istanbul*. London 1956. A readable, general account of the Christian and Turkish city.

CUDDON, J. A., *The Owl's Watchsong. A Study of Istanbul*. London 1960. A modern account of the city, quoting widely from earlier travellers.

RICE, DAVID TALBOT, *Constantinople: Byzantium – Istanbul*. (Photographs by Wim Swaan.) London 1965. Traces the whole history of the city: well illustrated with a useful short bibliography.

SHERRARD, PHILIP, *Constantinople. Iconography of a Sacred City*. Oxford 1965. A more metaphysical account with considerable quotations from contemporary authors. Illustrated.

EYICE, SEMAVI, *Istanbul. Petit Guide à travers les monuments byzantins et turcs*. Istanbul 1955. A most useful, though unfortunately scarce, handbook produced for the tenth International Congress of Byzantine Studies at Istanbul.

Much information on recent work in the city can be found in the volumes of Dumbarton Oaks Papers and in the reports of the Byzantine Institute on the uncovering of the mosaics in Hagia Sophia. Paul Underwood has just published in three volumes an authoritative account, *The Kariye Camii* (London 1967): R. Van Nice is producing a detailed account of the church of Hagia Sophia, which will amplify the work of E. H. Swift (1940). Cyril Mango has discussed some problems of the Great Palace in his *The Brazen House* (Copenhagen 1959).

For reference, the two volumes of R. Janin: *Constantinople Byzantine* (2nd edn: Paris 1964) and *Géographie Ecclésiastique de l'Empire Byzantine: Tome III* (Bucharest 1953) are invaluable.

THE TURKISH PERIOD

EGLI, ERNST, *Sinan: der Baumeister Osmanischer Glanzzeit*. Stuttgart 1954.

PENZER, N. M., *The Harem*. Revised edition, London 1966.

ÜNSAL, BEYCET, *Turkish Islamic Architecture 1071–1923*. London 1959.

VOGT-GÖKNIL, U., *Living Architecture: Ottoman*. London 1966.

Sources of Illustrations

Most of the photographs used in the plates are my own. I am grateful to the Turkish Embassy and the Turkish Publicity Department for Nos. 10, 55, 60, 64 and 65; to the Walker Trust, University of St Andrews for Nos. 28–30 showing mosaics in the Great Palace (one of which figures also on the dust jacket); and to Thames & Hudson for providing Nos. 20, 23 and 37 from their archives. No. 2 is reproduced from Miss Pardoe's *Beauties of the Bosphoros* (1839) and No. 22 from Grelot's *Relation Nouvelle d'un Voyage de Constantinople* (1680); both were made available by the Bodleian Library, Oxford.

The line drawings used for Figs. 2, 4, 6, 9, 14–16, 20, 22 and 23 are from the Thames & Hudson archives. The maps and plans, figs. 1, 3, 17, 18 and 21, were drawn by Mr H. A. Shelley from my sketches. Figs. 7, 8, 10 and 12 are sketches by my son Mr David Maclagan, based on Canon Charles Curtis: *Broken Bits of Byzantium* (1891); Fig. 11 was also drawn by my son, and is based on an illustration in the Second Report of the Walker Trust (1958). Figs. 13 and 19 are based on J. Arnott Hamilton: *Byzantine Architecture and Decoration* (1933).

THE PLATES

4

5

6

7

8

9

11

12

13

14

15

16

17

18

19

23

26

27

28

29

30

33

34

35

36

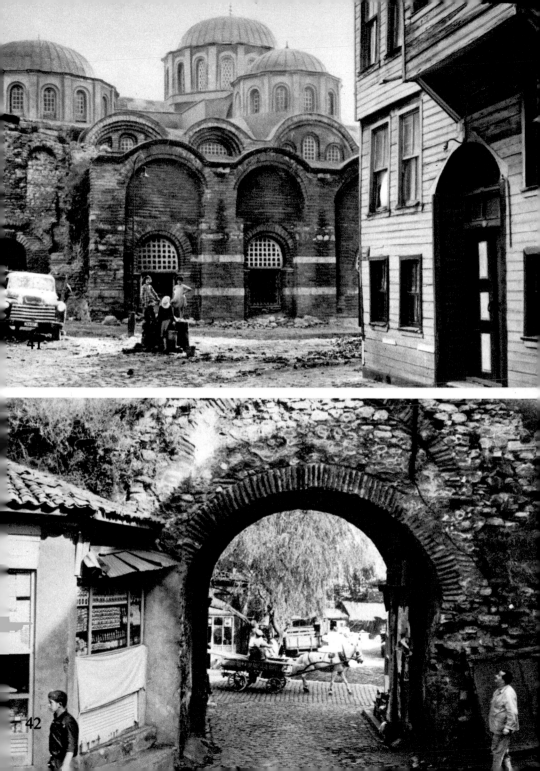

41

42

43

44

45

46

47

48

49

50

51

54

55

56

57

58

59

60

61

64

5

66

67

Notes on the Plates

1 The date and origin of this elegant column are alike uncertain. The inscription only has the words:

FORTUNAE REDUCI OB DEVICTOS GOTHOS

By some accounts it was occupied by a stylite hermit in the tenth century.

2 Column of Constantine, also called the Burned Column. Originally the column had nine drums of porphyry, the joins of which were concealed by gilt metal wreaths. There was a chapel with relics at the base About AD 330.

3 Aqueduct of Valens. Begun in AD 368. The mosque on the left, that of Fatih (the Conqueror) stands on the site of the great Byzantine church of the Holy Apostles.

4 This column, which now stands outside the museum, is closely related in style to the arch of Theodosius I; it must have come from that, or a very similar work.

5 Pillars of triumphal arch of Theodosius I. The nature of the pattern is obscure: some believe it to represent peacocks' feathers, others describe it as 'tear-drops'. A similar piece of column stands outside the museum. c. AD 390.

6 Fragment of column of Theodosius I, AD 396. Now embedded in the wall of the Hammam (bath) of sultan Beyazıt II.

7 This pillar of the arch seems to be gripped by a giant hand. The symbolism is uncertain. c. AD 390.

8 The Golden Gate. Almost certainly erected by Theodosius I. The inscription read:

HAEC LOCA THEVDOSIVS DECORAT POST FATA TYRANNI
AVREA SAECLA GERIT QVI PORTAM CONSTRVIT AVRO

If the association with the suppression of Maximus in 388 is correct, the date is about AD 390.

9   Carving on south face of base of obelisk of Theodosius I: the Emperor and his court in the Hippodrome. *c.* AD 390.

10   Egyptian granite obelisk set up at Karnak by Thutmose III 1471 BC. Erected in the Hippodrome by Theodosius *c.* AD 390. Similar obelisks have found their way to London ('Cleopatra's Needle'), Rome and New York. In the background is the Mosque of Sultan Ahmet (Blue Mosque).

11   Land walls. Erected by the prefect Anthemius for Theodosius II AD 413.

12   Detail of walls: the round tower on the left is part of the addition of AD 447.

13   Corner of tower of land wall, showing construction with brick and ashlar on outside and concreted rubble within.

14   Capital, now outside Archaeological Museum, dug up at site of St Polyeuktos. It is identical in style and dimensions with two capitals on freestanding piers just south of St Mark's at Venice, hitherto reputed to have come from Acre. AD 524-7.

15   North arcade of church of St John of Stoudios. AD 463.

16   Floor paving in church of St John of Stoudios, *c.* AD 1290.

17   This charming detail of the pavement is in the north-west angle of the nave of St John of Stoudios. AD 1290.

18   Bucoleon palace. Loggia, with vanished balcony, opening on to sea, which then reached base of wall. Perhaps eighth century.

19 Sea wall with blocked arch, which probably once gave access for small vessels to the foot of a ceremonial stairway.

20 Hagia Eirene from Hagia Sophia. Sixth century. In the background can be seen a tower and other buildings of the Saray complex.

21 Interior of Hagia Eirene. Sixth century. This church never became a mosque, so there is no re-alignment of the east end.

22 Interior of Hagia Sophia, from Grelot. Visitors were not allowed in earlier Turkish times, and Grelot disguised himself; in consequence this engraving for some time gave the western world its idea of the church/mosque.

23 Interior of Hagia Sophia from west gallery. AD 532–7.

24 Hagia Sophia: capitals in south-west exedra of gallery.

25 Hagia Sophia: giant pillars of green Molossian stone on north of nave.

26 Gigantic capital, dug up in Topkapı Sarayı. This probably crowned a now vanished column somewhere in the neighbourhood.

27 Basilican cistern (Yerebatan Sarayı). Mid sixth century.

28–30 These mosaics are among those discovered on the site of the Great Palace during the excavations of the Walker Trust. Their dating is a matter of considerable controversy but they probably belong to the latter part of the sixth century AD. It seems likely that this section of the Palace was reconstructed after a relatively short period of use.

31 Tower of sea walls (fifth century) repaired by Theophilus in ninth century. The inscription on the lower stone course runs (in Greek): 'Tower of Theophilus Emperor in Christ'. The sea formerly came up to the foot of the wall.

32 Porphyry sarcophagi outside Archaeological Museum. The second from the right may be that of Julian the Apostate. Probably from church of the Holy Apostles. Fourth-fifth centuries.

33 Walled-up archway of Sancaktar Hayrettin Mescidi, an unidentified Byzantine church; converted into a Turkish prayer-house, now a dwelling. Not untypical of minor Byzantine monuments. Perhaps eighth century.

34 Bodrum Camii. Traditionally identified with church of Myrelaion. The upper church (shown here) probably dates from first half of tenth century.

35 Fenarî Isa Camii. Probably the monastery founded by Constantine Lips. Brickwork at east end of south church. About AD 1300.

36 Gül Camii. Probably church of St Theodosia. Decorative brickwork at east end. Possibly early fourteenth century.

37 Hagia Sophia. Mosaic of Constantine IX (Monomachus) and Empress Zoe. The Emperor wears state robes and carries an offering of gold in a purse. His head probably replaces that of an earlier husband of Zoe. The whole mosaic dates from about 1030 and the two heads from about 1050.

38 Hagia Sophia. Deesis mosaic in gallery. This combination of Christ between the Virgin and the Baptist is a common one in Byzantine art. Possibly early twelfth century (though an early fourteenth-century date also has supporters.)

39 Church of Christ Pantepoptes, the All-Seeing. Now a Turkish school (Eski Imaret Camii). It was the headquarters of Alexius V in 1204. Founded 1087.

40 Church of St John in Trullo (Ahmet Paşa Mescidi). Eleventh century.

41 Church of Christ Pantokrator, the Ruler of All. The two domes on the right belong to the southern church (last quarter of twelfth century) and that on the left to the later middle church (perhaps *c.* 1200).

42 Cibali gate in sea walls on Golden Horn. The original archway has been made smaller in Turkish times. It was a little to the north-west of this point that the crusaders broke into the city in 1204: this gate was the left flank of their attack.

43 Vefa Kilise Camii (probably the Church of St Theodore Tiro). Exterior from south-east. *c.* AD 1100.

44 Mosque of Arap Camii. This building in Galata on the north of the Golden Horn was originally the church of the Dominicans. It can be seen that although the masonry shows Byzantine influence, the arch is gothic. Middle of thirteenth century.

45 Vefa Kilise Camii. Earlier marble slab incorporated into west front, perhaps in fourteenth century. Original date possibly sixth century.

46 Church of the Virgin Pammakaristos, the All-Blessed (Fethiye Camii). View of south side, as reconstructed in early fourteenth century.

47 Kariye Camii (Our Saviour in Chora). West wall of central space under dome. The richness of the recently cleaned marble can be seen clearly. The mosaic over the door is of the Dormition of the Virgin. Early fourteenth century.

48 Tekfur Sarayı. View of great hall from interior courtyard. The richness of the brickwork suggests a fourteenth-century date.

49 Tekfur Sarayı. Exterior view of the other, outer side of the same building.

50 Rumeli Hisarı. General view of the 'Castle of Europe.' 1452.

51 Rumeli Hisarı. This battlement niche, with a Turkish slab at base and a Byzantine capital on the right shows the extensive re-employment of older materials. The whole castle is said to have been built in four months.

52 Murat Paşa Camii. One of the earliest mosques in the captured city. It is constructed of alternate courses of stone and brick. About 1470.

53 Fortress of Yedikule (Seven Towers). Built in 1457 by Mehmet II (the Conqueror). Originally the towers had conical caps. The wooden house in the foreground is a typical Turkish dwelling.

54 This handsome eighteenth century fountain stands by the Mosque of Kılıç Ali Paşa.

55 Turkish tiles in the Harem of Topkapı Sarayı, products of the most brilliant period of the factory at Iznik (Nicaea).

56 Turkish tiles outside the chamber in the Saray which houses the relics of the Prophet.

57 Mosque of Beyazıt II from the top of the tower of Beyazıt. The mosque was built 1501–5: the tower is nineteenth-century and is now in the precinct of the University.

58 Mosque of Süleyman I from the top of Beyazıt Tower. 1550–7. The Golden Horn can be seen in the background.

59 Rüstem Paşa Camii. General view of interior. This enchanting little mosque is lavishly decorated with faience tiles. 1561.

60 Ramazan Efendi Camii. Superb tiles of sixteenth century. This delightful little mosque was built in 1586 for Hacı Hüsrev Ağa: Ramazan was a later divine associated with the site.

61 Burmalı Minare Mescidi. A typical small foundation. too modest to boast a dome. The minaret has spiral brick decoration, unique in Istanbul.

62 Azapkapısı Camii. An octagonal mosque, built on the north shore of the Golden Horn by Sinan in 1577 for the Grand Vizier Sokollu Mehmet Paşa. In the background can be seen the Galata Tower, partly enclosed in scaffolding.

63 Kılıç Ali Paşa Camii. A late mosque by Sinan (1580) built for an admiral. The extension to hold the *mihrab* is an unusual feature. In the foreground the tomb of the founder.

64 Mosque of Sultan Ahmet I (Blue Mosque) 1609–17. On the right can be seen the site of the Hippodrome. In the foreground is the domed *türbe* of Sultan Ahmet himself. The whole area of the mosque and the football pitch in front of it was part of the site of the Great Palace of the Byzantine Emperors.

65 Mosque of Sultan Ahmet I. Interior. 1609–17.

66 Yeni Cami (New Mosque or Mosque of the Dowager Sultana). Begun 1597, finished 1663.

67 Wooden Turkish houses behind the sea walls. Most of Constantinople in the eighteenth and nineteenth centuries was filled with houses of this type. Fires were frequent.

Index

NOTES:
1. The Turkish letters Ç and Ş are listed as though they had no diacritical marks.
2. Subjects should be sought under the special headings: Churches – Cisterns – Columns – Councils – Emperors – Empresses – Forums – Great Palace – Heresies – Mosques – Sultans – Walls

192